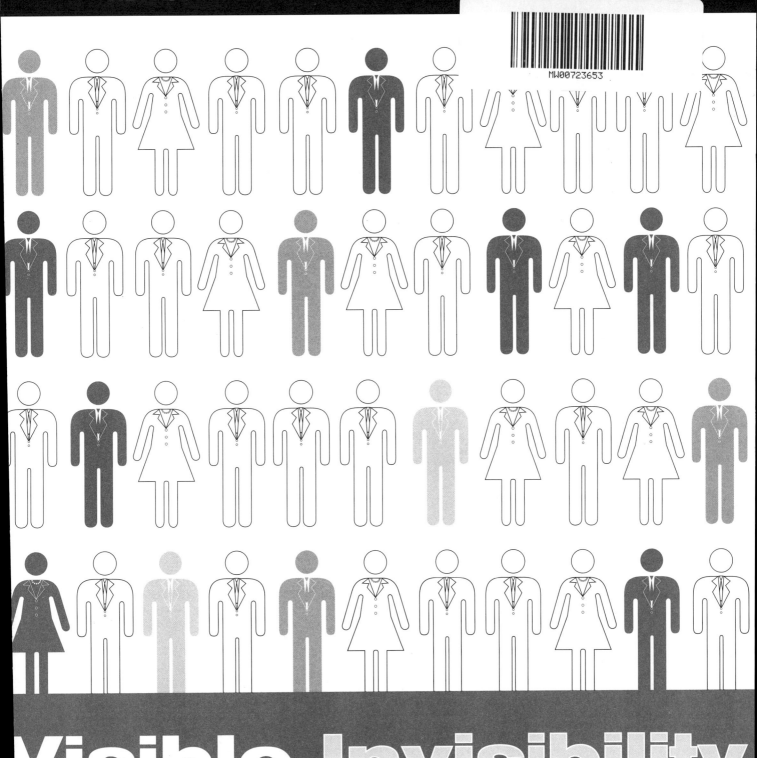

Visible Invisibility

Women of Color in Law Firms

AMERICAN BAR ASSOCIATION
**Defending Liberty
Pursuing Justice**

Prepared for the Commission by
Janet E. Gans Epner, PhD

COMMISSION
On
WOMEN
In The
PROFESSION

The Commission on Women in the Profession

Chair
Pamela J. Roberts

Members

Amelia H. Boss
Paulette Brown
Jana Howard Carey
Bettina Lawton
Raymond L. Ocampo, Jr.
Angela E. Oh

Arin N. Reeves
Lauren Stiller Rikleen
Gloria E. Soto
Hon. Elizabeth S. Stong
Robert N. Weiner

Board of Governors Liaison
Don S. De Amicis

Commission Liaisons

Leslie M. Altman
Linda A. Baumann
Phyllis G. Bossin
N. Kay Bridger-Riley
Kristy A.N. Bulleit
Hon. Cheryl Cesario
Jamir Couch
Pamela Chapman Enslen
Mary Chojnowski
Peggy A. Davis
Anne E. Dewey-Balzhiser
Leslie A. Farber
Sally Foley
Marcia D. Greenberger
Phoebe Haddon
Nancy Hoffman
Kathleen J. Hopkins
Heather D. Jefferson
Marylee Jenkins

Kim R. Jessum
Linda A. Klein
Renee M. Landers
Anne Lukingbeal
Kathleen M. McDowell
Anita Podell Miller
Judith A. Miller
Hon. Susan M. Moiseev
Jean Moyer
Jean Pawlow
Aileen A. Pisciotta
Estelle H. Rogers
Lynn Hecht Schafran
Jana Singer
Patricia Costello Slovak
Patricia M. Vaughan
Lish Whitson
Patricia H. Wittie

Staff
Veronica M. Muñoz
Staff Director

Tamara Edmonds Askew
Programs & Projects Manager

Julia Gillespie
Special Projects Coordinator

Barbara Leff
Communications & Publications Manager

Jennifer Gibb
Projects & Meeting Assistant

American Bar Association
Commission on Women in the Profession
321 North Clark Street
Chicago, IL 60610
Phone: 312/988-5715
Fax: 312/988-5790
Web Site: www.abanet.org/women

Marc Bendick, Jr., Ph.D.

Paulette Brown, Project Co-Chair

Kimberlè Williams Crenshaw

J. Cunyon Gordon

Rosita Lopez Marcano, Ph.D.

Peggy Nagae

Angela E. Oh

Nashra Rahman

Radhika Rao

Arin N. Reeves, Ph.D., Project Co-Chair

Judith Resnik

Veta Richardson

Joyce Sterling, Ph.D.

Sheila Thomas

Suzanne Townsend

David Wilkins

Angela F. Williams

Contributors

The ABA Commission on Women in the Profession thanks the following for their financial grants and contributions, which made this research initiative possible:

$75,000 +
Ford Foundation (Grant)

$50,000 - $74,999
Paul Hastings

$25,000 - $49,999
Levi Strauss (Grant)

$10,000 - $24,999
American Bar Association Section of Litigation
Baker Botts L.L.P.
Foley & Lardner LLP
Fulbright & Jaworski L.L.P.
Shell Oil Company

$5,000 - $9,999
Bernstein, Shur, Sawyer & Nelson P.A.
Epstein Becker Green Wickliff & Hall, P.C.
Latham & Watkins LLP
O'Melveny & Myers LLP
Vinson & Elkins LLP

$2,500 - $4,999
American Bar Association Section of Antitrust Law
Blank Rome LLP
CDW Corporation
Drinker Biddle & Reath LLP
Fine, Kaplan and Black, R.P.C.
Hays, McConn, Rice & Pickering, P.C.
Howrey LLP
Kirkpatrick & Lockhart LLP
McGlinchey Stafford PLLC
Morgan, Lewis & Bockius LLP
Morrison & Foerster LLP
Pepper Hamilton LLP
Schnader Harrison Segal & Lewis LLP
State Bar of California
Wolf, Block, Schorr & Solis-Cohen LLP

$1,500 - $2,499
Abrams Scott & Bickley, L.L.P.
Arnold & Porter LLP
Beirne, Maynard & Parsons, L.L.P.
Brown Sims P.C.
Buchanan Ingersoll & Rooney PC
Chamberlain, Hrdlicka, White, Williams & Martin
Connelly Baker Maston Wotring Jackson LLP
ConocoPhillips Company
Cozen O'Connor
Duane Morris LLP
Eckert Seamans Cherin & Mellott, LLC
Fox Rothschild LLP
Haynes and Boone, LLP
Marshall, Dennehey, Warner, Coleman & Goggin
Marshall & Lewis, LLP
McCarter & English, LLP
Montgomery, McCracken, Walker & Rhoads, LLP
Pillsbury Winthrop Shaw Pittman LLP
Reliant Resources Foundation
Saul Ewing LLP
Seyfarth Shaw LLP
Sheppard, Mullin, Richter & Hampton LLP
Stradley Ronon Stevens & Young, LLP
Willig, Williams & Davidson
Winstead Sechrest & Minick P.C.
Winston & Strawn LLP
Waste Management, Inc.

Host Firms
Ballard Spahr Andrews & Ingersoll, LLP
Southern California Edison

Despite our best efforts, we inadvertently may misspell or omit a name. We sincerely regret any such errors and greatly appreciate being informed of them so that we can correct our records. To report any mistakes or oversights, please contact the ABA Commission on Women in the Profession at 312-988-5715.

CONTENTS

Most private firm business models continue to adhere to the "pay your dues and climb the ladder" tradition. Regardless of how accomplished a woman may be, she cannot climb—much less reach the top of—the leadership ladder unless she spends a certain amount of years in her work environment. Nowhere is this more painfully obvious than with women of color in law firms.

Women of color experience a double whammy of gender *and* race, unlike white women or even men of color who share at least one of these characteristics (gender or race) with those in the upper strata of management. Women of color may face exclusion from informal networks, inadequate institutional support, and challenges to their authority and credibility. They often feel isolated and alienated, sometimes even from other women.

Previous research focused specifically on either women or on people of color in the legal profession. Recognizing the need for a comprehensive analysis of the unique concerns and experiences of Hispanic, African-American, Native American, and Asian-American women in the legal profession, in 2004 the Commission on Women in the Profession undertook a two-part research study, composed of a national survey and focus groups.

The study explores the experiences of women of color who had worked in a law firm of at least 25 attorneys, and it attempts to answers such critical questions as: Do their work experiences surpass or fall short of expectations? How do legal employers hinder or increase job satisfaction? Why do women attorneys of color change practice areas and organizations, or leave the profession at an alarming rate?

The report is not an end unto itself. It is a tool for law firm managing partners to implement change so that they retain women of color and enable these women to join the ranks of leadership. Women of color must be visible at all levels within private firms. If the legal profession is to move forward and reach its full potential, then it must reflect the diversity of society. Anything less is unacceptable.

> The report is . . . a tool for law firm managing partners to implement change so that they retain women of color and enable these women to join the ranks of leadership.

Pamela J. Roberts
Chair
ABA Commission on Women in the Profession

Law firms in recent years have appropriately expanded the scope of their diversity efforts from recruiting to also focus on retention and advancement of lawyers of color and women. On the surface, it seems like we are headed in the right direction—that is, until we take a closer look at one particular group of lawyers located at the intersection of race and gender: women of color.

Paulette Brown

The experiences, challenges, and career trajectories of women of color have never been fully understood before by just looking at either race or gender. Until the Commission on Women undertook this study, women of color in law firms have been consistently invisible and often ignored in spite of many of the diversity efforts under way in law firms. Our progress on diversity generally has been slow, but our progress with women of color has been even slower. What the findings of this study really demonstrate is that the combination of being a racial and a gender minority has a particularly devastating effect on women of color's personal and professional lives, and we, as a profession, have to step up to understand this situation better and do something about it. Across the board—whether we are talking about opportunities for advancement, integration into the social fabric of a law firm, or being compensated for one's efforts—the study's findings illustrate that women of color fare worse than women in general or men of color. And, women of color are the farthest removed from the successes of white men, who still tend to have the greatest levels of success regardless of where they went to school or their grades in law school. As law firms seek to become more competitive by having the best and

brightest of the available talent, they have to have an understanding of the talent drain that is occurring in their women of color ranks. It is truly time to make these women visible again so that their talents can contribute to the growth and prosperity in our profession.

Arin Reeves

Before undertaking this study, we knew generally what we were going to find, but the depth to which women of color are experiencing and being negatively impacted by their experiences in law firms was not only surprising, it was a jarring wake-up call even to those of us who deal with this issue in our own lives. We are not just losing talent; we are treating talented people in ways that do not speak well of our profession or the values that undergird it.

It is the intent of this study to serve as the first step in a very long conversation about these issues. For the purposes of creating a research study that was manageable in scope, we limited it to women of color in law firms. The issues for women of color lawyers obviously are not limited to just law firms. Women of color in the public sector, in solo practice, and in corporations also need to have their concerns brought to light and addressed. So, we do recognize the limits of what this study accomplishes, and we hope that it spurs further conversation and action. In addition, we hope

> Women of color in the public sector, in solo practice, and in corporations also need to have their concerns brought to light and addressed.

that this research is used by law firms to take a hard look at their practices. We have included recommendations that we believe will help law firms create the changes necessary to include women of color in their ranks of successful lawyers.

It has been our pleasure to work on this project, and we offer our deepest gratitude to all the voices and hands that have shepherded this project thus far. We thank the current and former Commissioners of the Commission on Women who gave so generously of their time and passion, especially the women who conceived the idea for this project. We are so very thankful to the amazing Com-mission on Women staff who have kept this project on track. We would also like to give thanks to the Advisory Board, which provided invaluable guidance throughout this project, and the numerous sponsors who provided the much-needed financial resources critical to the project's completion. This report is truly the result of the tremendous commitment and hard work of many brave souls, and we are grateful to each and every one of you.

Paulette Brown Arin N. Reeves, Ph.D.
Project Co-Chairs

In 1872, Charlotte E. Ray became the first African-American woman admitted to the bar in the United States. Despite her renowned legal abilities, she had to give up the practice of law because, as a woman of color, she could not attract sufficient clients to stay in business. The legal profession has changed dramatically since Ms. Ray practiced law, although many of the challenges she faced then still confront us today. Almost half of the associates in private law firms are now women and 15% are attorneys of color, but in 2004 only 17% of law partners were women and only 4% were attorneys of color. In the late 1990s, the National Association of Law Placement (NALP) found that more than 75% of minority female associates had left their jobs in private law firms within five years of being hired, and after eight years the percentage of those leaving rose to 86%. By 2005, 81% of minority female associates had left their law firms within five years of being hired.

Unfortunately, the NALP data tell us only part of a complex story. This report on the ABA Commission on Women's Women of Color Research Initiative goes beyond the NALP data to further our understanding of the professional lives of women of color and their experiences in law firms. It is an outgrowth of work done in the 1990s by the Multicultural Women Attorneys Network and the American Bar Association (ABA) Commission on Women in the Profession, in conjunction with the Commission on Racial and Ethnic Diversity. In that report, *The Burdens of Both, The Privileges of Neither,* women attorneys of color described the ways in which the combination of being an attorney of color and a woman was a double negative in the legal marketplace. This led the ABA Commission on Women to launch its "Women of Color in the Legal Profession Research Initiative" in 2003, a comprehensive study of the unique experiences and concerns of women of color in private law firms that included a national survey and focus groups.

This report represents the culmination of that study. In the survey component, male and female lawyers from majority and minority backgrounds were asked about their career experiences, salaries, and decisions to stay in law firms or to leave for other milieus. The responses of women of color were compared to those of white men, white women, and men of color to determine how their careers differed from those of their peers and the magnitude of those differences. Men of color and white women served as a frame of reference, indicative of the career impact of having one minority status instead of two. The national survey included men and women of color who were African-American, Native American, Hispanic/Latina, Asian, or of mixed background. The focus groups, comprised only of women of color, provided a more detailed picture of the career experiences of women attorneys of color and an opportunity to understand from their perspective how and why their career experiences differed from their counterparts. Information from the survey and focus groups were melded into a complete portrait of the career dynamics of women attorneys of color.

The ABA Commission on Women engaged the National Opinion Research Center, a social science research organization at the University of Chicago, to design and implement the survey and focus group methodology used in this study. Overall, 920, or 72% of all attorneys who were eligible to participate in the survey, returned a completed questionnaire. The response rate was 74% for women attorneys of color, 68% for men of color, 79% for white women, and 64% for white men. Focus groups were held in Chicago, New York City, Los Angeles, Atlanta, and Washington, D.C. Four focus groups were comprised of women attorneys of color from the same racial/ethnic background; one had women of color from diverse racial/ethnic backgrounds.

The career experiences of women of color in this study differed dramatically from those of their peers and from white male counterparts in particular. Nearly half of women of color but only 3% of white men experienced demeaning comments or harassment. Unlike white men, many women of color felt that they had to disprove negative preconceived notions about their legal abilities and their commitment to their careers. Seventy-two percent of women of color but only 9% of white men thought others doubted their career commitment after they had (or adopted) children.

Nearly two-thirds of the women of color but only 4% of white men were excluded from informal and formal networking opportunities, marginalized and peripheral to professional networks within the firm. They felt lonely and deprived of colleagues with whom they could share important career-related information. Women of color had mentors, but their mentors did not ensure that they were integrated into the firm's internal networks, received desirable assignments (especially those that helped them meet required billable hours) or had substantive contacts with clients. Sixty-seven percent of women of color wanted more and/or better mentoring by senior attorneys and partners, whereas only 32% of white men expressed a similar need.

Women of color often became stuck in dead-end assignments, so that as third- and fourth-year associates, their experience lagged behind their white male counterparts, limiting their advancement potential and career trajectories. Forty-four percent of women of color but only 2% of white men reported having been denied desirable assignments. Differential assignments, in turn, affected the ability of women of color to meet the number of billable hours required of them. Forty-six percent of women of color but 58% of white men were able to meet required billable hours.

> Women of color stated that they met with clients only when their race or gender would be advantageous to the firm.

Forty-three percent of women of color but only 3% of white men had limited access to client development opportunities. Women of color stated that they met with clients only when their race or gender would be advantageous to the firm; they frequently were not given a substantive role in those meetings. This kept them from developing business contacts that they could use to develop a book of clients or as resources for finding subsequent positions.

Nearly one-third of women of color but less than 1% of white men felt they received unfair performance evalua-

tions. Sometimes their accomplishments were ignored by the firm or were not as highly rewarded as those of their peers; sometimes their mistakes were exaggerated. Many women of color complained that they received "soft evaluations" which denied them the opportunity to correct deficits and gain experiences that could lead to promotions and partnership. Twenty percent of women of color but only 1% of white men felt they were denied promotion opportunities.

Salary was a high priority for women of color in the study; more than 70% were the sole or primary wage earner in their household—as were 81% of white men. Salary differences between majority and minority attorneys were not statistically significant, but attorneys of color made less money than their white counterparts.

In addition to these career hurdles, women of color in the survey and focus groups felt they could not "be themselves"; they downplayed and homogenized their gender and racial/ethnic identities. Some tried to act like the men in their firms, become "one of the boys"; others played down their femininity and tried to "mannify" themselves. The effort to minimize the impact of their physical differences was stressful to many women of color, an added burden to the long hours and hard work demanded by their firm. Many complained that they often felt invisible or mistaken for persons of lower status: secretaries, court reporters, paralegals.

The stress of second-class citizenship in law firms led many women of color to reconsider their career goals. The retention rates of women of color and white men reflected their lopsided experiences: 53% of women of color and 72% of white men chose to remain in law firms. Many women of color left firms to work in settings (especially corporations) that were lucrative, where they thought others' decisions about their careers would be less idiosyncratic, based more on merit, and where they had more flexibility to balance personal life, family, and work.

The careers of white women attorneys and men attorneys of color were neither as disadvantaged as those of women attorneys of color nor as privileged as those of white men. Fewer men attorneys of color indicated that discrimination had hobbled their careers compared to white women. However, white women, on average, had higher salaries than men of color (but the differences were not statistically significant). Men attorneys of color and white women had similar perceptions of how they felt others judged their competencies, their desire for more and better mentors, their rates of being selected as protégés by white men, and their desire to become partners in law firms. However, their retention rates were very different: 67% of white women but only 52% of men of color chose to remain in law firms.

Charlotte Ray would surely look at the number of women of color in the legal profession today and see how far the profession has come since she practiced law over a century ago. But, after taking a closer look at the experiences of women of color in the profession she might wonder just how much progress has been made after all.

RECOMMENDATIONS

Based on the research from the focus groups and the survey, the ABA Commission on Women proposes the following recommendations for law firms that we think will be of use to you as you work on integrating women of color fully into your diversity efforts. Because every firm is different, we recommend that you take the following suggestions and make them your own to ensure the greatest success. This list of suggestions is also not intended to be exclusive of other strategies that may be successful and necessary in getting your firm to address these issues in a way that works best for you. We encourage you to be inclusive, creative, and diligent in creating and sustaining diversity and professional development strategies that foster the successful careers of women of color.

Before you utilize the recommendations presented below, first assess the totality of your diversity initiatives and whether women of color are integrated into those initiatives. If your firm already has a thriving diversity initiative that has been integrated into the overall business strategic plan, make sure that women of color are fully integrated into that effort. This study clearly evidences that if women of color are not viewed as separate from women in general or people of color in general, your ability to recruit, retain, and advance them is impaired. When women of color are acknowledged as a unique group with unique needs within your larger diversity and professional development efforts, you are more likely to see the kinds of successes that we all know are possible. If your firm does not already have a diversity initiative, then ensure the integration of women of color as the initiative is being developed and implemented.

NOTE: These recommendations are based on the research from the survey and focus group components of the ABA Commission on Women's Women of Color Research Initiative and are focused primarily on what law firms, as institutions, can do to increase the presence and success of women of color in their attorney ranks. We are currently finishing a supplement to this research focusing specifically on women of color who have reached notable levels of success in law firms, and we will be publishing strategies for women of color on how to succeed in law firms when this supplemental research is completed.

1. Address the success of women of color as a firm issue not a women of color's issue.

2. Integrate women of color into existing measurement efforts.

3. Integrate women of color into the firm's professional fabric.

4. Integrate women of color into the firm's social fabric.

5. Increase awareness of women of color's issues through dialogue.

6. Support women of color's efforts to build internal and external support systems.

7. Stay compliant with anti-discrimination and anti-harassment policies and hold people accountable for noncompliance.

INTRODUCTION

In 1872, Charlotte E. Ray graduated from Howard University School of Law and became the first African-American woman admitted to the bar in the United States and the first African-American woman to practice law in Washington, D.C.[1] A solo practitioner with a specialty in corporate law, she was reputed to give "a clear, incisive analysis of . . . the most delicate legal questions."[2] Despite these accolades, the *Chicago Legal News* reported in October 23, 1897 that "[a]lthough a lawyer of decided ability, on account of prejudice she was not able to obtain sufficient legal business and had to give up . . . active practice."[3] Charlotte Ray moved to Brooklyn, New York, became a teacher, married, and died in 1911 at the age of 60.[3]

In 1900, there were 112,939 attorneys in the United States, of whom 718 were African-American and 81 were "colored," defined by the U.S. Census as Chinese, Japanese, Korean, or Indian men.[4] The U.S. Census did not include statistics on women lawyers at that time. Today, Ms. Ray would find a very different demographic profile of attorneys in the United States. In 2004, 50% of JDs were women and 21% were of a racial or ethnic minority.[5] By 2005, 49% of practicing attorneys were women, 6% were African-American, 2.6% were Asian, and 3.5% were Hispanic/Latino.[6]

If Ms. Ray, a lawyer "of decided ability" in her time, compared her experiences to those of women attorneys of color today, she would find that almost half (48%) of all associates in private law firms are women and 15% are attorneys of color. Despite this considerable change, she would be disappointed to learn that in 2004 only 17% of law partners were women, and only 4% were attorneys of color.[7] She would undoubtedly be disheartened to discover that the careers of women of color today parallel her career: *In the late 1990s, more than 75% of minority female associates had left their jobs in private law firms within five years of being hired and, after eight years, the percentage of those leaving rose to 86%. By 2005,*

81% of minority female associates had left their law firms within five years of being hired.[8]

Ms. Ray would probably wonder why the success rate and tenure of women of color in private law firms is so much worse than that of white women and males of all races and ethnicities—as do law firm managers who are losing their investment after hiring and training them. There is little data to shed light on this issue. The National Association of Law Placement (NALP) *Directory of Legal Employers*,[9] first published in 1971, contains detailed data on private law firms, but the data offer an incomplete demographic picture of the career status of women attorneys of color. The NALP data report the number of women attorneys (white women and women of color combined) and attorneys of color who are associates and partners in law firms. This makes it impossible to determine the number of *women of color* who are associates and the number who are partners because they are subsumed within the categories of "women" and "attorneys of color." The NALP data also do not describe separately the associate and partnership status for men and women attorneys who are African-American, Hispanic/Latina, Native American and Asian-American attorneys, or explain how and why women and lawyers of color become underrepresented at the partnership level.

This report begins to fill this gap. It is an outgrowth of work done by the Multicultural Women Attorneys Network, which was formed in the 1990s by the American Bar Association (ABA) Commission on Women in the Profession, in conjunction with the Commission on Racial and Ethnic Diversity. The Network hosted a series of six roundtable discussions with groups of women

> By 2005, 81% of minority female associates had left their law firms within five years of being hired.

1

lawyers from diverse racial and ethnic backgrounds throughout the United States in order to identify and assess the unique experiences, priorities, and needs of lawyers who, by the nature of their physical appearance, confront barriers associated with *both* race and gender. The Network also held regional conferences in New York City and San Francisco to continue gathering facts, to disseminate information, and to identify larger policy issues reflected in individual experiences. Each conference drew 150 to 200 participants.

The Multicultural Women Attorneys Network published their findings from the roundtables and conferences in a report titled, *"The Burdens of Both, The Privileges of Neither."* Women attorneys of color in that study reported that "the combination of being an attorney of color and a woman is a double negative in the legal marketplace, regardless of the type of practice or geographic region involved."[10] They felt "ghettoized" into certain practice areas and felt a need to continually establish their competence to professors, peers, and judges. They felt invisible in the profession and reported experiencing greater difficulty attaining prominence and rewards in legal practice. Women attorneys in that study also reported facing gender discrimination in bar associations of color and race discrimination in majority bar associations.[11]

These findings led the ABA Commission on Women to launch its Women of Color in the Legal Profession Research Initiative in 2003, a comprehensive study, which included a national survey and focus groups, of the unique experiences and concerns of women of color who have worked in private law firms of at least 25 attorneys. The purpose of the national survey was to determine which factors had an impact on the career opportunities and trajectories of attorneys and their decisions to remain in or leave private practice. Surveys were sent to white men, white women, men of color, and women of color, all of whom were lawyers. Their experiences provided a frame of reference for comparing the experiences of women attorneys of color.

Five focus groups were held to clarify the results of the survey and get a more detailed understanding of the dynamics that impede or enhance the careers of women attorneys of color. Of the five focus groups, four were attended by women attorneys from the same racial/ethnic background; one was attended by women of color from diverse racial/ethnic backgrounds. (Details about the survey and focus groups appear in Section III and in Appendix B.) The research questions addressed in the survey and focus groups are described in the following section.

Research Questions

1. Is there a difference in success (salary, career achievement) for women attorneys of color in law firms, measured both quantitatively and qualitatively, compared to white men, white women, and men of color?

2. How do women of color compare their experiences in law firms to those of white women, men of color, and white men? How much of their experience can be understood as being affected by race, gender, or the combination of race and gender?

3. What are the retention and attrition rates for women of color in law firms, and why do women of color leave law firms? Do their reasons for leaving law firms differ from those of white men, white women, and men of color?

4. Where do women attorneys of color go when they leave law firms, and why are these destinations more attractive to them than law firms?

5. What strategies do women of color in law firms use that lead to perseverance and success? Do these strategies differ from those of white men, white women, and men of color?

6. What strategies does the Commission on Women recommend that law firms use to increase the retention of women of color?

Overview of This Report

This report begins with a description of the methods used to collect information from attorneys in the two components of the study, the survey and focus groups. It is followed by a profile of attorneys in the survey: their age, gender, marital status, educational background, years spent practicing law, the size of the law firm in which they worked, the number of employers they have had, and current employment status. These characteristics were taken into account in the analysis in order to understand the unique effects of race and gender.

In the longest section of this report, the career experiences of women of color are compared to those of their colleagues. As will be seen, many women of color had little difficulty making the transition from law school to their first job in a law firm, but once hired, they experienced incremental and cumulative disadvantages in their careers. These disadvantages included: finding an effective mentor, becoming integrated into internal networks, having access to relationships with clients, and receiving assignments that led to the development of practice skills and client contact, particularly those that helped meet required billable hours. Salary disparities between women attorneys of color, men attorneys of color, and white attorneys, both men and women, are also examined. The impact of incremental and cumulative disadvantages provides the backdrop for understanding the job satisfaction and career choices of women of color, along with their efforts to balance career demands and marriage and family.

The report concludes with recommendations for law firms interested in recruiting and retaining women attorneys of color.

Terms Used in This Report

The phrase "of color" used throughout this report is an umbrella term for persons who are Hispanic/Latina, African-American, Native American, Asian-American, and those from multiracial backgrounds.

African-American and Black are used interchangeably to describe persons who identify themselves as having origins in the non-white racial groups of Africa.

Asian-American and Asian refer to persons who identify themselves as having origins in East Asia (for example, Japan, China, Korea), South Asia (for example, India), Southeast Asia (for example, Vietnam, Philippines), or as Pacific Islanders.

Hispanic/Latina refers to persons of Latin American descent, including but not limited to Mexico, Central America, South America, and Puerto Rico.

Native/American Indian/Alaska Native refers to persons who identify themselves as coming from this background. Because of the small number of Native women in legal practice and to protect their

identity, the report does not distinguish between American Indian and Alaska Native attorneys or those from Indian reservations or Alaska Native villages.

Indian law refers to the specific practice of law regarding legal documents and policies governing tribes having a unique relationship with the United States through treaties and other specific legislation. Alaska Native legal practice, in this report, is subsumed under the term "Indian law" in order to protect the confidentiality of participants.

Retention rate refers to the decision to pursue one's career in a private law firm; it does not necessarily imply retention in the same law firm.

Attrition rate refers to the decision to leave the private law firm for an entirely different work milieu, such as becoming a solo practitioner, working in a corporation, a nonprofit organization, etc.

Comments from respondents and focus group participants. Some attorneys in the survey wrote comments in response to the two open-ended questions at the end of the questionnaire. In the report, the comments by white men, white women, and men of color (none of whom participated in focus groups) are preceded by the word "wrote," as in "One white woman attorney wrote. . . ." A variety of terms are used to report comments made by women of color who spoke during the focus groups, such as "she said, described, explained, mentioned," etc.

Works Cited

American Bar Association, 2004. *JD Degrees 1984-2004 (Total/Women/ Minorities)*.

Curran, Barbara A. and Clara N. Carson, 2005. *The Lawyer Statistical Report: Growth and Gender Diversity, A Statistical Profile of the Legal Profession in 2000*. Chicago: American Bar Foundation.

Jones, Edward T. III, Janet Wilson James, Paul S. Boyer (eds.) 1971. *Notable American Women, 1607-1950: A Biographical Dictionary, Volume III*. Cambridge, Mass.: The Belknap Press.

Multicultural Women Attorneys Network, 1994. *The Burdens of Both, The Privileges of Neither*. Chicago: American Bar Association.

NALP Foundation for Law Career Research and Education, 2005. *Toward Effective Management of Associate Mobility*, Washington, D.C., National Association for Law Placement.

NALP Foundation for Law Career Research and Education, 2003. *The Lateral Lawyer: Why They Leave and What May Make Them Stay.*

Smith, J. Clay, 1993. *Emancipation: The Making of the Black Lawyer, 1844-1944.* Philadelphia, Pa.: University of Pennsylvania Press.

U.S. Bureau of Labor Statistics, Employment and Earnings, January 2006. Household Data Annual Averages, Table 11: Employed Persons by Detailed Occupation, Sex, Race, and Hispanic or Latino Ethnicity.

U.S. Census, *The Twelfth Census, Special Reports, Occupations Available (1904)*. "Total Males and Females Ten Years of Age and Over Engaged in Selected Groups of Occupations, Classified by General Nativity, Color, Conjugal Conditions, Months Unemployed Age Periods and Parentage: 1900."

Notes

1. Smith, J. Clay, 1993. *Emancipation: The Making of the Black Lawyer, 1844-1944.* Philadelphia, Pa.: University of Pennsylvania Press.

2-3. Jones, Edward T. III, Janet Wilson James, Paul S. Boyer (eds.) 1971. *Notable American Women, 1607-1950: A Biographical Dictionary, Volume III.* Cambridge, Mass.: The Belknap Press.

4. U.S. Census, *The Twelfth Census, Special Reports, Occupations Available (1904)*. "Total Males and Females Ten Years of Age and Over Engaged in Selected Groups of Occupations, Classified by General Nativity, Color, Conjugal Conditions, Months Unemployed Age Periods and Parentage: 1900."

5. American Bar Association, 2004. *JD Degrees 1984-2004 (Total/Women/Minorities)*.

6. U.S. Bureau of Labor Statistics, Employment and Earnings, January 2006. Household Data Annual Averages, Table 11: Employed Persons by Detailed Occupation, Sex, Race, and Hispanic or Latino Ethnicity.

7. NALP Directory of Legal Employers, 2004-2005, Washington, D.C., National Association for Law Placement.

8. NALP Foundation for Law Career Research and Education, 2005. *Toward Effective Management of Associate Mobility*. Washington, D.C., National Association for Law Placement.

9. NALP Directory of Legal Employers. Washington, D.C., National Association for Law Placement.

10-11. Multicultural Women Attorneys Network, 1994. *The Burdens of Both, the Privileges of Neither*. Chicago: American Bar Association, pp. 6, 9.

The Women of Color in the Legal Profession Research Initiative included both survey and focus group data collection and analysis. The purpose of the survey was to compare the career experiences, salary, retention and attrition of women attorneys of color to those of white men and women and men of color in law firms, and to determine the magnitude of differences. The purpose of the focus groups was to provide a more detailed picture of the career experiences of women attorneys of color and to understand, from their perspective, how and why their career experiences differed from those of their counterparts. These two sources of information were then melded into a complete portrait of the career dynamics of women attorneys of color.

The Commission on Women engaged the National Opinion Research Center (NORC) to conduct the survey and focus groups. NORC is a national research organization at the University of Chicago that conducts complex surveys as well as qualitative research. NORC survey resources include questionnaire design and survey methodology, telephone and Internet data collection and data preparation, a national interviewer field structure, database development, and quality control assurance. Together with the Commission on Women Research Advisory Board, NORC developed the questions used in the focus groups and recruited focus group participants. NORC conducted the focus groups and provided written transcripts to the Commission on Women.

In the social and behavioral sciences, focus groups are an important and legitimate source of data when specific conditions are met (as they were in the ABA Commission on Women study). First, the problem or issues to be addressed must be clearly defined. Second, focus groups should be composed of relatively homogenous participants. Third, the questions asked during the focus group must be carefully worded and decided upon prior to the focus group (the focus group interview schedule can be found in Appendix A). If there is more than one focus group, all groups should be asked the same set of questions. Fourth, the discussion should be guided by a facilitator trained to conduct focus groups. The facilitator's job is to ask for clarification if an item under discussion is confusing or ambiguous, ensure that all participants voice their views, and ensure that all relevant topics are covered in the time allotted for the focus group. A professionally run focus group is not "just" a discussion. Participants in a professionally run focus group do not have to reach consensus, nor do they necessarily have to disagree. The objective is to gain insight into a particular issue or problem. In this study, the survey data provided valuable information about "what" was happening in the careers of attorneys and the magnitude of problems or events—a skeletal structure of career dynamics. The focus groups provided valuable information as to the "why" and "how" of career dynamics, which added form and shape to the skeletal structure.

The Survey

The national survey included attorneys who at some point in their legal careers worked in a law firm of 25 attorneys or more. The questionnaire used in the survey was based on prior studies of gender and race issues, questions from the ABA membership application, and importantly, issues that emerged from previous ABA focus groups and conferences with women attorneys of color.

In the first section of the survey questionnaire, respondents were asked about their background (e.g., year of graduation from law school, class rank in law school, years of experience as a practicing attorney, and current employment status). In the second section, respondents were asked about hiring, advancement and attrition, hours worked, highest rank held, mentors, and the effect of spouse or family life on career changes and salary negotiations. Respondents were also asked what changes they would like to see made at their law firms (e.g., more and better attorney training, opportunities for pro bono work, etc.), their long-term career goals, their satisfaction with law as a career, favorable and unfavorable traits and skills they felt were attributed to them and, if applicable, reasons for leaving a law firm of 25 attorneys or more. (The 40-item questionnaire used in the survey can be found in Appendix A of this report.)

Attorneys eligible to participate in the survey were identified in two ways. The sample of women attorneys of color was drawn from a list of women attorneys of color who registered their interest and willingness to participate in a survey by going to a Web site hosted by the Commission on Women and providing contact information on the Web site. The sample of white men, white women, and men of color was randomly drawn from the ABA's Membership Database and restricted to those who had provided an e-mail address on their membership application. Only attorneys who had worked in a private law firm with at least 25 attorneys at some point in their career were eligible to participate in the survey.

In October 2004 the survey was sent to attorneys via e-mail. Attorneys are familiar and comfortable with that technology; they use it to communicate with clients and colleagues, and previous research has demonstrated that lawyers prefer this mode of communication. It is also cost-efficient. (A detailed description of the data collection, data processing, and data preparation activities used in the survey can be found in Appendix B.)

To preserve respondents' anonymity, survey questionnaires did not include names, nor were there any links between names and ID numbers. Each questionnaire included an identifier indicating whether the respondent was a woman of color, man of color, white man or white woman. This made it impossible to determine whether a specific individual returned a completed questionnaire, so all follow-up contacts to increase the survey response rate were sent to all eligible members of the sample.

Overall, 920, or 72% of all attorneys who were eligible to participate in the survey, returned a completed questionnaire. Response rates (including out-of-scope cases—see page 66) differed for each group in the sample. A total of 632 women attorneys of color participated in the survey, a response rate of 74%. There were 132 men of color, a 68% response rate; 194 white women, a 79% response rate; and 157 white men, a 64% response rate.

The Focus Groups

Five focus groups comprising women attorneys of color were convened in March and April 2005. The questions asked of focus group participants were divided into four sections. Participants were asked first to describe the process of being hired by a private law firm of 25 or more attorneys, as well as their professional development and career advancement in those firms, including training, work allocation and assignments, mentoring, and evaluations of performance and pay. They were asked next to compare their experiences to those of their counterparts, that is, white men, white women, and men of color. Focus group participants were then asked to evaluate the advantages and liabilities that their gender and race/ethnicity might have had on their career experiences. The fourth set of questions asked about formal and informal avenues for training and development in law firms and which worked best according to focus group participants. Focus group participants were also asked to describe changes that private law firms could make that would enhance the career success of women of color and about support they received from professional associations, family and friends. (A copy of the focus group protocol can be found in Appendix A.)

Attorneys who participated in the focus groups were recruited from three sources: survey respondents who asked to participate in a focus group, women attorneys of color who were not contacted to be in the survey but who indicated their interest in the research on the ABA Commission on Women Web site, and referrals from individual attorneys and national and local bar legal associations of color. None of the focus groups had more than one participant from the same law firm, and an effort was made to include participants who ranged in positions and years of experience as practicing attorneys.

A total of 48 women attorneys of color participated in the focus groups. Of the five focus groups, one was held in Chicago with 11 Hispanic/Latina women attorneys, another was held in New York City with nine African-American women attorneys, a third was held in Washington, D.C. with nine Native American women attorneys, and a fourth was held in Los Angeles with 10 Asian-American women attorneys. A fifth focus group was held in Atlanta with nine women attorneys of color from different racial and ethnic backgrounds.

II. A Profile of Survey Respondents and Focus Group Participants

Attorneys who participated in the survey and focus groups were asked questions about their background that could help to explain differences in career success other than race/ethnicity and gender. These included age, legal education, years spent practicing law, the size of the largest private firm at which they worked, the number of employers they have had, marital status, and current employment status. These characteristics were taken into account in the analysis of career experiences and attainment of lawyers in order to identify the unique effects of race/ethnicity and gender. For example, if the white men in the sample were older, on average, than women of color, then part of the difference in their salaries could be due to age and legal experience rather than gender or race/ethnicity per se.

Sixty percent of women of color who responded to the survey were African-American, 24% were Asian-American, 10% were Hispanic/Latina, less than 1% were Native American/Alaskan Native, and 5% identified themselves as multiracial. Among the 128 men of color who responded to the survey, 48% were African-American, 22% were Asian-American, 22% were Hispanic/Latino, 4% were Native American/Alaskan Native, less than 1% were Native Hawaiian or Pacific Islander, and 3% identified themselves as multiracial. Data from the survey were not analyzed separately for men and women from each racial/ethnic subgroup because the number of attorneys in each subgroup was too small to be statistically reliable.

(A detailed description of survey respondents can be found in Appendix C.)

Survey Respondents

Overall, the women of color in the survey were younger than the white men and white women. Half of the women of color were 35 years of age or younger compared to 11% of the white women and 8% of the white men. Half of the white women and white men in the survey were between 46 and 60 years of age as were only 11% of the women of color. An additional 24% of the white men in the survey were older than 60. Thus, it is not surprising that a larger percentage of women of color in the survey (41%) were associates or attorneys of counsel, compared to only 19% of white women and 20% of white men. (Twenty-three percent of men of color were associates or of counsel.) A larger percentage of white women and white men were partners or shareholders in a firm of 25 or more attorneys (46% and 52%, respectively), compared to only 12% of women of color. (Twenty-eight percent of men of color were partners or shareholders in a firm of 25 or more attorneys.)

Women attorneys of color were also more likely to work in larger private law firms. Nearly half (48%) of the women of color in the survey worked in firms with more than 450 lawyers, as did 24% of men of color, 29% of white women, and 30% of white men.

Fifty-seven percent of women attorneys of color graduated from a first-tier law school compared to 46% of men attorneys of color, 40% of white women, and 52% of white men. However, in terms of class rank, white women and white men were nearly twice as likely to have been in Law Review or the Order of the Coif as women or men attorneys of color. Few attorneys in the survey worked as a judicial clerk after graduating from law school, but 23% of women of color, 21% of men of color, 17% of white women and 18% of white men did so.

Fifty-six percent of women of color in the survey were married or living with a partner, compared to 80% of men of color, 81% of white women, and 89% of white men. Thirty-five percent of the women attorneys of color had never married compared to 14% of men attorneys of color, 8% of white women and 6% of white men. Divorce rates were also higher among women (8% of women of color and 10% of white women) than men (5% of both men of color and white men).

Focus Group Participants

In order to understand the range of experiences of women attorneys of color, NORC recruited younger and older women, relatively junior and more senior women, women who were married and women who were not, those who worked in law firms of fewer than 50 attorneys and those who worked in firms of more than 1,000 attorneys. Of the 48 focus group participants, six held an advanced degree other than a J.D.

Thirty of the 48 focus group participants were working as an associate or of counsel and 10 were employed as a partner or shareholder in a private firm. The other eight focus group participants were employed as in-house attorneys, in corporate legal departments, in the nonprofit sector or in a government office. The average age of focus group participants in all five cities was between 30 and 40 years old.

All of the African-American participants in the New York City focus group had also participated in the survey. The women in this focus group worked in the widest variety of employment settings: large law firms (where some were associates and some were partners),

smaller firms with fewer than 25 attorneys, corporations, and government offices.

The Hispanic/Latina attorneys who participated in the focus group held in Chicago worked in firms nearly twice the size of firms in the other focus groups.

The Asian-American attorneys in the Los Angeles focus group were older and held more senior positions than participants in other focus groups. All were employed full-time, and five of the 10 participants were employed as a partner or shareholder in a private law firm. Three held advanced degrees other than a J.D.

The Native American attorneys in the Washington, D.C. focus group were three years younger, on average, than the attorneys in the other focus groups and were employed mainly as associates or of counsel in private law firms.

Six of the 10 attorneys in the Atlanta focus group also participated in the survey. This was the only focus group that was not restricted to a particular race or ethnic group but instead was open to all women attorneys of color. Attorneys in the Atlanta focus group were, on average, five years younger than the focus group participants in other locations.

Attorneys in the survey were asked if they ever missed out on desirable assignments, networking opportunities, or opportunities to build relationships with clients, or were denied opportunities for advancement and promotion. They were also asked if they felt that these career-damaging experiences could be attributed to race or gender. *Less than 5% of white men reported ever having career-damaging experiences, and less than 1% of white women and white men who reported career-damaging experiences attributed them to race.* Among attorneys of color, however, a much different picture emerged:

- 29% of women of color and 25% of men of color reported missing out on desirable assignments because of race.
- 49% of women of color and 31% of men of color reported that they were denied informal or formal networking opportunities because of race.
- 35% of women of color and 24% of men of color reported having missed client development and client relationship opportunities because of race.
- 16% of women of color and 19% of men of color reported that they were denied advancement and promotion opportunities because of race.

When asked whether career-damaging events could be attributed to gender, *less than 3% of white men or men of color attributed such experiences to gender.* Women attorneys in the survey told a much different story:

- 32% of women of color and 39% of white women reported missing out on desirable assignments because of gender.
- 46% of women of color and 60% of white women reported that they were denied informal or formal networking opportunities because of gender.

- 32% of women of color and 55% of white women reported having missed client development and client relationship opportunities because of gender.
- 14% of women of color and 28% of white women reported that they were denied advancement and promotion opportunities because of gender.

These women understood that exclusion from networking opportunities, desirable assignments, client relationships and promotion opportunities would limit their career trajectories within law firms. At first glance, it appears that white women experienced greater gender-based career problems than women of color. However, it is important to bear in mind that women of color experienced career disadvantages based on race *in addition to* gender, while white women experienced disadvantages based on gender alone. The combined disadvantages of race *and* gender among women of color explain at least in part why law firms have less success retaining women of color than either men of color or white women.

In addition to experiencing combined disadvantages due to race and gender, women of color found that their career disadvantages were cumulative. For example, being denied desirable assignments kept them from broadening and honing their legal skills and put them at a competitive disadvantage (with white men especially) after they had been with the firm for a few years. The negative career dynamics they experienced in law firms and attributed to race and gender deterred many women of color from pursuing careers in law firms.

> . . . it is important to bear in mind that women of color experienced career disadvantages based on race *in addition to* gender, while white women experienced disadvantages based on gender alone.

Juggling Gender and Racial Identities in Law Firms

Most women of color in the survey found it stressful to negotiate their gender and racial identities in a predominantly white, male environment. Nearly half (49%) reported having been subjected to demeaning comments or other types of harassment while working at a private law firm, as did 47% of white women, 34% of men of color and only 2% of white men. An Asian attorney recalled:

> I had a managing partner call me into his office when I was a fourth year [associate]. He introduced me to the client, who was Korean, and he tells him that I'm Korean too. He says, "She eats kim chee just like you." He said to me, "Talk to him." I looked at the client and said, "It's a pleasure to meet you. I'm sure you speak English better than I speak Korean." The client's face was so red. Then the partner left a message on my internal message system and he was speaking gibberish, trying to sound like an Asian speaker. I called every partner on my floor and said, "You need to come and listen to this." I played that message ten times. Ten times.

A Native American woman said:

> You have to have an incredibly tough skin. . . . I had people make comments like, "Oh, you're Indian. Where's your tomahawk? Are you going to scalp me?" Or, "Can I call you Pocahontas?" . . . When I was called "chief" and brought it to people's attention I was told, "Oh, you're spoiling [our work] environment here." So I had to leave.

Women of color in the focus groups described their efforts to fit into the culture of the law firm, but they did not think that their white male counterparts experienced or understood how difficult it was for them to do so. (Data from the survey confirmed their suspicions; less than 3% of white men reported having experienced any form of discrimination.) As one African-American woman explained: "Being a racial and gender minority in a fairly large firm is a constant culture shock that requires me to constantly play the role of a race- and gender-neutral person in an attempt to 'fit in.'"

Some women of color tried to fit into law firms by becoming "one of the boys." An African-American woman attorney said, "I noticed that the white women acted like the guys—very bold, upfront, strong and forthcoming. So I acted like the guys too. And if you do things like the men in my office do, they regard you as one of the guys." An Asian woman said, "I think there's a mystique about the Asian woman: we're so cute and so delicate, we're sexual vixens in bed. You get to the point where you try to 'mannify' yourself." The effort to behave in ways that did not come naturally to them but that they thought would be acceptable to the white men in their firms left many women of color feeling stressed and alienated from life in the law firm.

Several women of color described how others caricatured them based on both gender *and* race, such as the African-American attorney who heard herself described as "an angry Black woman" or the Asian attorney who heard herself described as a "dragon lady." These incidents reminded women attorneys of color of their "otherness," that they did not, in fact, "fit in" in an environment where being white and male were the norm. An Asian attorney recounted, "I've had opposing parties, opposing counsel, treat me like a little girl and part of that is the Asian thing because they see a little Asian doll . . . it's really annoying and I'm tired of it."

Another Asian attorney said:

> I get so many comments because I'm Asian, I'm a woman, and I look young. They try the first-year associate thing, they try the honey thing, they ask where are you from, you speak English so well, you don't even have an accent. . . . When I first started practicing it would make me incensed to the point where I would lose my concentration and focus and I would not be as good of an advocate as I would have been if it weren't an issue. But now I see that as part of their war chest of possible weapons to try to disarm me and shake me up.

Although women of color juggled both racial and gender identities in law firms, they sometimes found that gender was a bigger problem than race. An African-American woman said, "African-American males were much more readily accepted [at my firm] than were females." A Latina commented, "There's definitely this machismo that goes with being a corporate lawyer. . . . In the law firms where I have worked the first hurdle is being a woman on the corporate side. After that, being a person of color. It's worse being a woman."

Most women of color in the survey reported having experienced some form of race- or gender-based discrimination, but a few women of color—especially some of the light-skinned women in the focus groups—did not think that their race or ethnicity had a negative impact on their career. A Latina commented, 'This [phrase] "woman of color" is something I'm not comfortable with because I never considered myself 'of color.'" A Native woman attorney said, "My firm probably didn't even know I was Native when they hired me. I work on Native American policy and I'm pretty well known for doing that, but I don't primarily practice in that area. They're happy I'm there, but I don't think that it factors into how I'm treated at all." An Asian-American attorney saw no difference between herself and white attorneys at the law firm. She explained, "My parents were born in Vietnam, I was born here, but I never really grew up around other Asian-Americans. I don't really a see a difference between my Asian-ness and their Caucasian-ness." Another Asian-American woman commented that some stereotypes of Asian women were advantageous. She was a partner in a law firm and explained:

> The more senior you get, the more freely other partners will talk to you about their stereotypes, and they have a very positive stereotype of Asians, and especially Asian women. They see us as hard-working—we'll work seven days a week, 24 hours a day; we're very smart, very dedicated. One of the Asian women who recently made partner just had twins, and they're sure she'll keep working, while they think other women would quit.

However, these women were exceptions. Most women of color in the survey and focus groups found that being a woman and a member of a racial minority group made it more difficult to become integrated into the law firm, created career hurdles that white men did not experience, and proved to be emotionally draining.

Recruitment: Law School and the Transition to Practice

To help understand the attrition of women of color in law firms, it is useful to compare their recruitment experiences with their career experiences once they begin working in law firms. Attorneys in the survey were asked to identify all the avenues they used to find their first (and subsequent) positions in law firms. Women of color relied more heavily than other law school graduates on the on-campus interview; 46% found their first job this way compared to 28% of men of color, 36% of white women, and 24% of white men. Women of color also relied more heavily on summer clerkships than white men, men of color or white women (33%, 20%, 21%, and 30%, respectively.) Twenty-nine percent of women of color used the law school's placement office to find their first job, as did 17% of men of color, 22% of white women, and 23% of white men.

It is not clear how to evaluate differences in the strategies these attorneys used to find their first job in a law firm, particularly the heavier reliance on campus interviews and summer clerkships among women of color. It is possible that law firms found on-campus interviews to be an efficient method for finding and recruiting women of color. It gave them a chance to talk with candidates and it gave women of color a chance to learn about the firm. Similarly, it is possible that law firms and women of color used summer clerkships to evaluate how satisfied each one was with the other. It is possible that law firms did not need to go to such lengths to identify and recruit other groups of attorneys. (Twenty-eight percent of men of color relied on on-campus interviews to find their first job in a law firm; 21% were hired following a summer clerkship and 18% submitted unsolicited resumes. Thirty-six percent of white women used the on-campus interview process; 30% were hired following a summer clerkship and 22% used the law school's placement office.)

Strategies used by white men to find their first job in a law firm were more evenly divided between on-campus interviews (used by 24% of white men), the law school's placement office (used by 23% of white men), and summer clerkships (used by 20% of white men).

Most women of color in the focus groups found that their gender and racial/ethnic background were assets in getting hired by a law firm. As one Latina explained, "Being a minority does help you get the job. I'm finding that firms and corporations all want, on paper, the statistics that they've hired a diverse population."

Some women of color reported that they were "strategic hires," that is, hired for presumed skills such as fluency in Spanish or Chinese, ties to a specific local clientele, or to show the legal community that the firm values and employs women and lawyers of color. An Alaskan Native attorney explained:

> I got hired for my firm's American Indian law and policy practice . . . and because of the contacts that I had in the Native American community, and because I'm a lobbyist on the Hill. So I think that my race helped me. I think being female helped me because I think they were trying to diversify the practice.

Although their status as a racial and gender minority may have helped them get a job in a law firm, some women of color experienced racial hazing during job interviews. One African-American woman reported:

> I was interviewing with one of the bigger firms and the guy interviewing me was an English major. So was I. He asked me who my favorite poets and writers were and I mentioned a few African-American writers. After awhile he said, "If you can recite a T.S. Eliot poem, I'll give you an offer right now." I couldn't, but I thought okay, file this one away for the books.

Some women attorneys of color suspected that law firms held different standards for lawyers of color and majority candidates, and that the standards for lawyers of color were higher than those for white lawyers. One woman of color stated:

> Most of the white associates [at my firm] went to state schools, but all the minority associates were from the top ten law schools. If you're not from a top ten law school and you're a minority candidate, you're not on the same playing field as a white applicant from any law school.

In sum, many women of color found that their status as a racial and gender minority was an asset in the hiring process. Nearly half of all women of color in the survey found their first job as a result of an on-campus interview, perhaps because law firms found it an efficient means to identify and recruit women applicants of color with a particular academic pedigree. Some women of color reported that law firms hired them to forge business relationships with clients from the same background as the woman of color. Though most women of color had positive experiences during the hiring process, some suspected that law firms held them to a higher standard than their white peers, and some reported disconcerting race- and gender-based remarks. Once hired, women of color found that race- and gender-based advantages quickly disappeared, leaving them to confront serious career hurdles, one of which was the lack of effective mentoring.

Mentors and Protégés

The attorneys in this study, whether newly hired or more experienced lateral hires, recognized the importance of having a mentor and the downside of not having one. Sixty-seven percent of women of color in the survey wanted more and better mentoring by senior attorneys and partners, as did 52% of men of color, 55% of white women, and 32% of white men. A Latina explained:

> Law firms work like a patronage system. If you don't have someone watching out for you, you'll fall through the cracks. It's very hard to find a mentor if there's not somebody who identifies with you. Either you have the same likes or you come from a similar background or you can talk about your school or something to draw a connection. And for a lot of people of color and for a lot of women, there isn't anyone in the partnership, in the upper echelons, that has a similar background or can empathize with you or relate to you and therefore, you don't end up having a mentor.

Another Latina said, "[You need to] have a mentor from the very beginning to look out for you to make sure you don't get stuck on huge document reviews and to make sure that you get good work. People pick

Table 1: Attorneys Who Received Formal and/or Informal Mentoring by Race of Mentor

Mentor	Formal Mentorship				Informal Mentorship			
	Women of color protégée	Men of color protégé	White women protégée	White men protégé	Women of color protégée	Men of color protégé	White women protégée	White men protégé
One or more women of color	5%	1%	1%	0%	27%	10%	4%	1%
One or more men of color	4%	2%	0%	1%	29%	18%	4%	8%
One or more white women	20%	5%	8%	6%	41%	21%	43%	29%
One or more white men	24%	29%	21%	31%	49%	71%	67%	74%

their protégés really quickly, and if you're left out it's going to be really tough for you."

Many law firms acknowledge that mentoring is an important aspect of attorney development and have implemented formal mentoring programs that match mentors and protégés, or they assign new hires to work with one or more partners or senior associates. Forty-three percent of women attorneys of color reported having had formal mentors, as did 26% of white women, 32% of men of color, and 31% of white men.

However, most women of color in the focus groups agreed that while formal mentoring programs were good in theory, truly effective mentoring occurred when mentors and protégés formed relationships more naturally. An Asian woman attorney explained, "Mentoring can't be forced. I got the impression I was interfering with my [white male] mentor and it became a chore [for him] more than something he wanted to do." Another woman of color found formal mentoring programs off-putting. She said, "My firm recently decided to start an official, formal mentoring program that's only going to be for minority associates and I think it's disgusting. The moment they announced it, I thought it was so wrong for so many reasons . . . like we're in Special Ed."

Most attorneys in the survey reported that they were chosen as protégés by senior attorneys through informal processes. Eighty-three percent of women of color, 77% of men of color, 81% of white women, and 78% of white men reported having had informal mentoring relationships. When asked about the gender and racial/ethnic background of their mentors, most attorneys reported that they were mentored by one or more white men (see Table 1), but women of color were *least* likely to have been informally mentored by white men.

Seventy-four percent of white men and 71% of men of color were informally mentored by white men, as were 67% of white women and only 49% of women of color. *This difference may be a critical differentiating factor in the careers of men and women, and especially women of color.* If white men and men of color have better-connected, more powerful mentors than women (and women of color in particular)—mentors who cultivate their skills more carefully—one would expect them to have greater career success.

Women of color in the focus groups welcomed opportunities to work with white men who took an interest in their careers and helped groom them for success. One woman of color recalled:

I worked in a small firm and one day I got a call out of the blue from an older Jewish partner and . . . we just hit it off. Had I stayed it would have been the kind of thing where everyone would know that I'm going to be a partner because he was taking care of me and making sure I developed correctly and that's how it should work. It defies color and gender; really it's just the luck of the draw.

A Latina told this story:

There was a [white] partner who, unfortunately, died of cancer. But he made it a point to get to know every single associate regardless of whether they were a minority or not. And he spent time with them and offered assistance and put them in departments and made them part of teams, and then followed up, discussed with the partner who was supervising, and he was really good at it and was very human about it. But there's no way to replace him, unfortunately.

Another woman of color described how her career blossomed as a result of support she received from the men in her firm:

Although I worked primarily in an all-white-male firm, the attorneys, partners and associates were very supportive of advancing my career. I had the opportunity early on to be assigned to accounts that let me develop client relationships, which have helped me establish my own practice. The key was finding a senior associate who was on the cusp of partnership and then becoming part of his team. I was young and therefore not a threat and had incredible opportunities to grow along with him. I was offered partnership, ultimately. . . .

> Some white men who reached out to mentor women had limited success advocating on their behalf.

Some white men who reached out to mentor women had limited success advocating on their behalf. A white male attorney in the survey wrote:

As a group head I had difficulty getting proper salary increases for female litigators in my group. I also had great difficulty having them promoted to partner. I noted that even when females were made partner, they were never put on management committees or given any real leadership prerogatives.

The fact that they were less likely to be mentored by white men, coupled with the difficulty some white men in the survey reported when they tried to advocate for women of color, illustrate how dynamics within law firms limit the career potential of women of color in law firms.

Just over 40% of women of color and white women reported that they were informally mentored by white women. Twenty-seven percent of women of color and 4% of white women were informally mentored by a woman of color. (Twenty-two percent of men of color and 29% of white men were informally mentored by white women and 10% of men of color and less than 1% of white men were informally mentored by a woman of color.)

When focus group participants were asked whether they preferred men or women as mentors, one woman of color said, "I would feel more comfortable with a female mentor than a male mentor, but she doesn't necessarily have to be a minority." A Latina attorney said, "I'd much rather work for women than men. I feel much more comfortable asking questions of women partners than the male partners." A Native American woman attorney said, "Both of my female mentors are minorities, the partner and the of counsel. And I have great relationships with them. That's been most helpful to me . . . I reach out to them for advice on getting assignments and getting development."

When asked about working with senior women attorneys, a few women of color described generational clashes; some found them callous or competitive instead of collaborative. A Native American woman said, "In my firm the women are really mean. I get mentored by these women and I hate it. . . . Women partners don't have a lot of power so they can't really help you or stand up for you in the firm. They expect you . . . to suck it up and don't have a lot of sympathy." Other women of color found that senior women simply did not have the time to mentor younger female associates. A Latina attorney observed, "Women who are more senior who are in positions of power usually don't have time to mentor young attorneys. They want to and they have really good intentions and you may have a lot in common with them but . . . they've got to run home to be with their kids. And I can understand that."

Twenty-nine percent of women of color, 18% of men of color, 8% of white men and 4% of white women were informally mentored by men of color. When asked about working with men of color, an African-American woman observed, "I think minority males have the attitude, 'I made it this far on my own with nobody helping me, why should I help anybody else?'" Another African-American woman said:

> There was one black partner and he definitely focused on the black male summer associates and the black male summer potential hires. . . . He ignored the black women . . . I find that black male partners tend to get very excited about potential black male hires in part because they feel they can mentor them fully without any suspicion about the relationship. They can engage them fully in their practice and socially, whereas I don't think that they embrace black women to same degree during the hiring process and when you first get there.

One woman of color pointed out that some male African-American mentors lack sufficient power within the firm to advocate successfully on behalf of protégées:

> I work for an African-American partner and he gives me advice and tries to pull me along. But he was a lateral hire and I'm not sure if he's familiar enough with the process of navigating up the ranks in the firm. Even though he's an equity partner, I'm not sure if at the end of the day he could make me a partner.

On the other hand, some women of color reported having excellent rapport with male mentors from the same ethnic background. A Latina said:

> I was recruited by a Hispanic male who was a very successful person in the firm and he was my mentor. He recruited me, brought me in for the interviews and really opened a lot of doors. [He] also got me involved in bar associations at the local level and talked about client development and doing all the things that [make a difference in career success]. And it really makes a huge difference.

Women attorneys of color were well aware that regardless of race or gender, powerful mentors were better able to help their protégés advance within the firm. One Latina observed:

> There are Caucasian males who will reach out and try to mentor you and they will do their best. And it depends on how powerful they are in the firm and how much work they have as to whether or not they'll be successful. There are a limited number of people who are willing to do that; there are not enough of them and there's not enough time for all of the people who need mentoring. So people fall through the cracks, and it's usually us.

An African-American woman recalled:

> When I was hired there were four black attorneys. We were all under the same senior partner and we realized that he was the weakest link in the firm and there were efforts to get rid of him. So we all left because there was no way that you could move anywhere [inside the firm].

When discussing why mentors hesitated to choose them as protégées, some women of color in the focus groups reported that they were considered to be "flight risks," to leave because of family demands or because another firm hired them. A Latina put it this way: "As a partner, you say, 'Okay, I've got a choice here. I can either go with this guy or I can go with this girl, and where am I ultimately going to have the greatest return?'" An African-American woman lawyer said:

> An apprenticeship takes investment on the part of the partners to train and develop associates, to really know what they're doing. They're going to make that investment selectively and they're going to make it in people they think will be there for the long term and not leave after three or four years.

A Latina attorney commented:

> The pressure is not just on associates, it's on partners as well. They have to bill a lot more than they used to, and I think they have less time for client development and . . . to reach out and mentor. As a result, if something requires extra effort they may not have the time to do it. Since it takes extra effort to connect with and look

out for people of color and women, it makes it a lot easier for us to fall through the cracks.

Senior women attorneys of color in the focus groups who wanted to mentor associates described the considerations they had to take into account when choosing protégées. A Latina partner reported that her firm could not retain women associates of color and that their attrition was burdensome. She said:

We hired a woman, she was terrific and she had great credentials. We spent about two years training her and she had a baby and then she left. We're not a big firm so that was a big expense. Another woman came around, we spent two and a half years training her and then she got married, had a baby, and then she left. My partner said, "You know, it's illegal, you're not allowed to say it, but the next time a woman comes through here, don't even bring her into my office. I'm not going to interview her." It's only after women attorneys get older that men figure that you're going to be around.

Another senior attorney of color commented that her firm asked her to recruit woman and minorities and integrate them into the firm. As she put it:

For several years . . . I felt that the burden of diversifying the firm was placed on my shoulders. The firm now has seven other attorneys of color, both male and female, but as the only shareholder of color I still feel I have to look out for everyone [who is a minority attorney]. I think it is easier on the firm as a whole to avoid dealing with diversity issues because I am there.

An Asian partner described her role in mentoring Asian women attorneys and the steps she has taken to minimize attrition:

I grab all the Asian women. Our firm pays for a mentor lunch every month so I grab each of the women I'm mentoring and we go out to lunch together for a one on one. I'll ask them "What's going on, what's bugging you, do you feel we're doing enough to further your career, what do you want to know about what's going on with the firm?" Just really connect with them so I can make sure that I have a good handle on where are they with respect to the firm and nobody's going to quit tomorrow and say, "Oh, by the way, I was really unhappy."

While having a mentor does not guarantee career advancement and success in a law firm, becoming a partner typically requires having a sponsor who will groom the individual for partnership. Effective mentors in law firms initiate new attorneys into the practice of law and provide experiences required for career advancement. They offer associates assignments that sharpen their legal skills and help them meet required billable hours, and they help associates develop business relationships with clients and the community more generally. They monitor their protégés closely and provide them with feedback about their performance.

Mentors of color are role models insofar as they represent what minority associates of color can achieve in the firm. Some women of color thought that having attorneys in the top echelons of the firm would improve their career opportunities at the firm. As one Latina put it, "Until the top changes, we're not going to see a whole of success for people [of color] as they [try to] get to the top. The difficulty for us minority associates is that we cannot find minority role models that we can look up to."

Women of color observed that powerful mentors were able to protect their protégés during economic downturns. A Latina attorney said, "I managed to keep my job [during the recession of the late 1990s] because I was lucky enough to find a mentor who was very well-connected and who was going to make sure that I wasn't going to be one of the people let go."

Regardless of the race or gender of the mentor, the critical issue for women of color is whether they derive the same benefits from mentor-protégé relationships as their white and male counterparts. Those benefits include being integrated into firm networks, receiving assignments that meet billable hours and lead to career advancement as well as client development, and being offered opportunities to specialize in areas of law that interest them. To the degree that women of color lack mentors who can provide them with these experiences, their career choices and trajectories will be more limited than those of their counterparts. The two-thirds of women of color who wanted more and better mentoring by senior attorneys recognized how vital good mentors were to attorneys' career success in law firms.

Internal Networks

Becoming integrated into internal networks is critical to career success within law firms. One woman of color described how the "otherness" of women of color in law firms led to their exclusion from internal support networks, which in turn undermined their career advancement:

Most people are not overtly racist or sexist and do not believe that they are racist or sexist. However, by human nature, we tend to be more comfortable with those with whom we can identify and share similar background and interests. In private law firms, this can make a huge difference because of the general "free market" nature of associating with others to work on cases, refer clients, etc. *To survive in private practice, you not only need to excel at your trade, you also need a strong support network within the firm. It is this second component that is typically lacking for women attorneys of color.* (emphasis added)

Sixty-two percent of women of color in the survey reported being excluded from informal or formal networking opportunities, as did 60% of white women. Thirty-one percent of men of color and only 4% of white men reported similar problems.

An African-American woman described her experience:

I came to my firm through the summer associate program. One of the things I remember most starkly was how quickly the white men became indoctrinated into the culture of the firm. We had many activities and the white male summer associates interacted very quickly with the partners and they created bonds not only based on work, but socially and outside of work as well. There really wasn't that opportunity for women in general. It carried over very distinctly into

our first-year associate experience, and that translated into work assignments and attention from certain partners. . . . Because of these preexisting relationships, work groups and client relationships were established quickly [and those] relationships continued throughout our careers.

A woman of color in the survey wrote:

I am often excluded from opportunities for informal mentoring and information sharing—the lunches and happy hours and golf outings between male and Caucasian attorneys. These informal settings allow majority attorneys to get valuable insight, "dirt," and work opportunities. This information leads to better work, more client contact, etc. Being left out puts me at a disadvantage compared to majority attorneys.

Most women of color attributed their exclusion to the persistence of the "old boys' network" in their law firm. Some thought men of color could penetrate the old boys' network, some did not. A woman of color commented, "White males prefer minority males to female attorneys. I think it's a comfort zone; the law is still a very male-dominated business. And their comfort level is to deal with other males. I've seen it in our headquarters and in our branch office." A Native American woman said, "I don't think they liked having non-white males around or non-white females who weren't into their jokes and everything. It's a very uncomfortable environment." (The fact that half as many men of color reported feeling excluded from the firm's networks as women of color indicates the greater ease they had becoming integrated into the firm's networks.)

One woman of color described the awkwardness she felt with her boss: "I have nothing in common with my boss. I can't go to lunch with him. If we go out for a drink he'll cross his arms and we'll make small talk, but it's never about the game or about family life. It's just, 'Oh, did you get that account?'" These experiences contrasted sharply with those of white male attorneys. One woman of color observed:

There's a guy in the litigation department who plays golf almost every weekend with a partner who has a huge corner office next to me in a completely different department. They just hit it off playing golf. Is that going to help him? Maybe not. Have I ever been asked to play golf? Nope. I probably won't be. Whether or not he has a mentor, he came in and was put on a team that's going to go to trial and he'll get great experiences. I'm certainly reaching out to everybody I know to get as much [quality experience as I can]. . . . I don't know of any white men who fell through the cracks. I think they have work opportunities if they want them. It's just harder when you're not picked right out of the gate.

Many women of color felt invisible, mistaken for clerical staff, court reporters, or paralegals, or treated as if they did not belong in the firm altogether. An African-American associate said that if a white male partner approached her and a male colleague as they walked together down the corridor, "He'd speak to the white male associate and he wouldn't see me. It's like I'm not there or he assumes I am part of the administrative staff or that I wouldn't expect to be spoken to. He just speaks to the person he's used to and doesn't worry about me." Invisibility is costly to professional careers; partners do not invest in those they do not even see.

> Invisibility is costly to professional careers; partners do not invest in those they do not even see.

One might expect a strong camaraderie to have developed between women of color and white women based on having to confront similar gender-based career disadvantages, but many women of color in the focus groups felt disconnected from white women. An African-American woman commented:

I never felt gender solidarity with a lot of the white women even though I saw that they were also having difficulty at the firm. White women had lunch and did things together. Black associates, male and female, tended to work together but there really didn't seem to be room to work on gender issues. So I felt that black women, women of color, and white women had very, very separate experiences.

Another African-American woman said, "The Caucasian women go to lunch every day or every few days. Once a month they reach out and ask if I would like to go out with them." Another attorney commented that in her firm "there are three black women and they're administrative. The [white] women in the firm don't have that much support and, as a black woman, I clearly don't have any. So it's difficult to do the job."

One African-American woman found herself "ghettoized" because she received work assignments only from African-American male partners. She said, "All the work I was given came from the Black partners. So I felt marginalized in a different way, like I couldn't work for anyone else."

The intense loneliness that resulted from being marginalized at her firm led one African-American woman to leave the large firm where she worked:

I just felt like I lived in a completely different universe. . . . I felt like I didn't belong there, even though they had a formal mentoring program which I participated in. It was one of the reasons why I left big firm practice . . . this tremendous sense of being alone at work every day and not seeing a way to have real professional relationships where I felt part of the group. I didn't think that that would develop in the future.

A few women of color struggled to overcome their marginalization in the firm. One Latina attorney said:

What worked well for me was learning male preferences. They like sports. And it sounds crazy, but I've learned about sports and that has opened many doors for me. I learned about college football and it's amazing. I don't need to be an expert; I just need to know enough to be able to say, "Yeah, they should fire the coach." I pick things that I find myself interested in. I'm not going to pick professional golf, I don't follow it, but I do know about Tiger Woods and Veejay Singh. At least that has broken down barriers so they could say to themselves, "Hey, she likes the stuff we like." Now I'm more than a dancing, spicy-food person. So then they start asking me questions. I'll look at their office, find something they have an interest in, ask questions and somehow get myself in the door. I'm taking control over my career.

An African-American attorney offered this advice:

If you ask, people are willing to share their experiences with you. But if you just take an assignment and go into your office and bill your 70-80 hours a week, you're never going know the things you need to know until you mess up.

Another woman of color in the survey wrote:

The experience is what you make of it. You have to be outspoken and take responsibility for your career because you can get "lost" in a big firm. People will underestimate you and the management of the firm will not expect you to stick around. If you are serious about your career and show initiative, you will get recognized and people will be supportive. You will find mentors you did not expect. My biggest supporters are white males, but it took a long time for them to notice me and I have sacrificed a lot for my career.

It is likely that the marginalization and isolation described by women of color would decrease if they had a stronger presence. Attorneys in the survey were asked how important it was to them to increase the racial and gender diversity in law firms. Eighty-seven percent of women attorneys of color, 58% of men of color, 61% of white women, and 27% of white men felt strongly that law firms should increase their racial diversity. Forty-four percent of women of color, 30% of men of color, 52% of white women, and 12% of white men felt strongly that law firms should increase their gender diversity. The relative lack of interest by white male attorneys in increased racial and gender diversity in law firms suggests a lack of awareness (at best) or callousness (at worst) to the negative career experiences and disadvantages of being a minority in a law firm, particularly with respect to networking.

External Networks

Like internal networks, external networks—relationships with clients, bar associations, and the community more generally—are critical to career success within law firms. A white male attorney in the survey wrote:

In both large and small firms, the key to success, the only sure route to both partnership and the upper partnership levels, is to control a significant amount of business. This means either inheriting responsibility for the firm's institutional clients or finding new clients, the latter being more difficult but more financially rewarding. . . . Having an expectation of becoming a partner and remaining a partner without controlling significant business is unrealistic. While all firms need good lawyers, such persons can be hired and need not be promoted to partnership as a reward for hard work. . . . It has been my experience with young attorneys working their way up through the ranks that this concept is not well understood. Almost all of them start out feeling and continue feeling for a long time that it is enough to come to work in the morning, bill time, and go home at night, without making the extra effort to bring in new business, entertain existing clients, and join and participate in bar association or community activities. Even when such persons become a partner in a firm, their tenure is not secure, as they do not control any business.

Among attorneys in the survey, 43% of women of color reported limited access to client development and client relationship opportunities, as did 55% of white women, 24% of men of color, and only 3% of white men. One woman of color said, "White men have a greater ability to network and gain clients because those clients look just like them. Women of color aren't seen as people to be taken seriously." A Latina struggled with how to handle her exclusion from client contact at her firm, despite having done a considerable amount of work on a case:

[The male associate or partner] wasn't trying to exclude me on purpose but it was still hurtful. For my career it was hurtful too. I thought, "Why am I not meeting the client we're working with?" It comes up a lot [but] . . . I don't really know how to address it. I don't want to seem too aggressive about it or that I'm being discriminated against; I don't want to give that impression. So I'm [trying] to be very strategic about the way I say it, but I haven't addressed it.

Women of color in the focus groups reported being treated like "show horses," brought to meetings to impress clients but without having a substantive role. One woman of color wrote, "When diversity was an asset to landing a government contract or eliciting new business from clients of color I was included in client meetings, but not otherwise." Another wrote, "Partners only introduce clients to women attorneys of color when the client is a person of color too."

Men of color in the survey wrote that they had similar experiences: "There were several cases that had parties of different races. I was asked to 'assist' in those cases simply by sitting at the counsel table. I did not get substantive experience. I was simply providing 'colorful' face time for the jury." A Native American man wrote, "Life for an American Indian man is very difficult at a big law firm, particularly for a new associate. . . . At the firm I was at, American Indian attorneys were expected to develop clients, but then not allowed to bill toward those projects because the work was doled out to white attorneys. Disgraceful."

One woman of color said:

I felt like an exotic animal. I was always asked to attend functions and award ceremonies, speak to law students of color, and pose for advertising publications. However, I never had contact with partners in power other than at these events. Law firms would do well to examine whether their associates of color are given *real* opportunities to interact with the power structure of the firm.

These stories illustrate that in order for external networking opportunities to produce career benefits, they must be coupled with meaningful, not token, professional assignments and relationships with powerful attorneys within the firm.

The importance of developing *ongoing* relationships with clients was also noted by women in the focus groups. An African-American woman explained:

If you have opportunities early on to form a continuing relationship with a client, you get increased responsibility over a period of time versus someone who bounces from client to client and from deal to deal, working with different people and not being able to build up that continuity of experience. After two or three years you're going to notice the difference in the level of responsibility and the level of experience that the person who has had continuity has achieved.

Clients' objections to working with specific attorneys were infrequent but 19% of white women, 15% of women of color, 14% of men of color and 3% of white men reported that clients asked to work with someone else. Despite being infrequent, when such requests were granted, they underscored the lack of support women of color felt from their law firms and exacerbated their lack of access to client relationships. One woman of color described her dismay when a case was taken away from her despite the client's *preference* for her representation:

A white male in my firm worked on a transaction from the beginning to just before the closing. He had to leave to get married and would be gone for two to three weeks on his honeymoon. So I stepped in and took over the closing. I worked with the client for one week. At the end of the deal the client said "Wow, you did a great job! We can forget about what's-his-name; I want you to be on our deals going forward." They had a deal in the pipeline and he mentioned it to the partner who was working on the deal. The client said, "I want [her] to work on this deal." Then the partner said, "Okay, we'll talk about that." Right away I could hear some reservation. On our way back to the airport the partner said, "Well, I understand that [the client] said he wanted you to work on his next transaction. We'll definitely find a way to get you involved, to a certain extent." I never did anything on the next deal, even though the client wanted me.

Some women of color experienced blocked access to clients when they tried to bring business into the firm based on their ethnic background but were discouraged from doing so. A Latina commented, "At my firm, I don't see a real effort to reach out to the Hispanic community and develop a law firm practice in those areas. My goodness; we're in a city where the Hispanic population is the number-one growing population of minorities."

An Asian woman described how disheartened she felt by the lack of support she received from the partners in her firm after she was harassed by a client:

We were at the printer's. They had a layout of food, all kinds of cuts of chicken, and the client had been flirting with me. He said, "I like my meat dark." I was so naïve, I said, "Oh, me too!" I didn't get it at all. So he's looking at me and says, "You know, I have yellow fever." At that point I realized he was being completely inappropriate and a total jackass. I went up to my partner and told him that the guy had made a racial comment and was hitting on me. His response? "Well, don't you find him attractive?" I went to the only female partner and her response was, "Just let it lie. Don't make waves, just move on."

In sum, women attorneys of color in the survey and focus groups found themselves marginalized and peripheral to life at their law firm. This left them feeling lonely and alienated from life at the firm, without colleagues with whom they could eat lunch or have a drink after work. Exclusion from internal networks meant that that they did not receive "inside" information about incoming cases, firm politics, strategies for advancement, or how to secure assignments that would hone their legal skills. They also reported having more limited opportunities to develop relationships with clients, particularly ongoing relationships, which in turn limited their career trajectories with the firm. Women of color attributed a good deal of their disadvantage to the reluctance of senior attorneys to work with them and their preference for working with other white men. However, women of color who worked in law firms where senior attorneys took an active interest in their careers and provided them with the tools and experiences they needed to be successful responded enthusiastically to the support they were given, and their careers blossomed as a result.

Skills and Training

Assignments are the building blocks of legal careers. At the bottom of the legal "assignment pyramid" are document reviews, legal research, and contributing to a brief. More desirable assignments include inter-

viewing witnesses and significant participation in a trial. At the top of the pyramid are assignments such as being the lead attorney on a trial and managing client relationships. Assignments in law firms are not distributed equally among associates, and 44% of women of color reported being passed over for desirable assignments compared to 39% of white women, 25% of men of color and 2% of white men. Forty-four percent of women of color wanted greater influence over their assignments as did 32% of men of color, 24% of white women, and 17% of white men. Fifty-four percent of women of color wanted to see less subjectivity in the allocation of work, as did 31% of men of color, 30% of white women, and 10% of white men. The relative nonchalance among white men with respect to the distribution of work assignments and subjectivity in the assignment process reflects their advantage in these areas. By contrast, women of color described how they got trapped in dead-end assignments early in their careers. One Latina said:

There were a bunch of law firms that were part of this huge document review project and [a member of one of the firms] asked me if my firm hired white people. . . . I wasn't sure why so many minorities [from my firm] had been put on a dead-end project that was going to last for a long time. I was the only Latina and there were two black women. We were all minorities.

Another woman of color wrote:

I was relegated to the cases that no one else wanted, I was limited to handling cases and working with other women and minorities almost exclusively, and I was denied access to the most influential and powerful people in the firm: eight white male partners.

A white female attorney echoed these sentiments. She wrote:

I worked in litigation. Women got more research and document review assignments. Men got more courtroom opportunities and more opportunity to interact with clients. Women often got assigned "workhorse" positions on large, lengthy cases; our work was valued but we did not get the same opportunities to do "live" activities such as taking or defending depositions.

An Asian woman explained how the perception that she was hard-working became a career liability:

> You don't get to leave your desk, you don't ever get to go out to take those depos, meet clients, make a court appearance, or interview a witness. They just don't let you out. They think you're great but they don't have a positive expectation of how you will interact with a client, a court, or anybody on the opposing side.

An African-American woman received a similar career-stalling compliment about her work product: "People would say to me, 'You have such good attention to detail; it saves me so much time.' So I felt like I was stuck in this 'you're doing great' work bubble when I wanted to stretch and try something new."

Women of color also described getting "pigeonholed," given assignments based on a presumed skill or interest. An Asian woman recalled:

> Somebody came into my office and asked me to look over a document in Chinese and I don't read Chinese except for like dim sum menus. I was asked and another woman was asked. But we had a white Jewish male attorney who read Chinese and he was not asked. He pointed out that if we're truly diverse and we're looking at skills, then they should have asked him too, which was an excellent point.

Another Asian woman reported, "They gave me a document in Korean and said, 'Can you read this?' And I said, 'This is Korean, I'm Chinese.' And they couldn't understand why I couldn't read it."

However, membership in a specific minority group occasionally led to plum assignments, as it did for an African-American woman attorney who commented, "I got pretty high-profile trials because even though the client was white, they wanted to present a black face because they knew the jury was going to be black and Latino. So race, in that respect, was helpful." Such examples among survey respondents and focus group participants were rare.

Some women of color in the focus groups learned to speak up for themselves and found that this helped them get better assignments. An African-American woman said, "You're going to get called for crap work and you have to take it sometimes, but then you also have to tell people what you want to do. Then you're more likely to get the work you want." Another African-American woman recalled, "We had a black male partner and I told him how much I hated an assignment, and he said that if I want to do intellectual property, I need to tell the partners and senior associates and the assignment partner, and I need to remind them. And that's what I did. I learned that lesson."

An African-American attorney described her transition from passively accepting assignments to actively seeking assignments:

> It took me six months to a year to learn that people weren't just getting their assignment, taking it, doing it and then waiting for the next one or calling and saying I need another assignment. It was an eye-opener to learn that people were jockeying for good cases or they'd hear about a case and approach the partner director. I was waiting to be assigned.

Another woman of color said, "[When I asked to] get off an awful assignment, the advice they gave me was to get busy on other things. You have to show that you've become invaluable on another case, which is basically what I did, and I've gotten great experience since then on a much smaller team." An African-American woman attorney described the cumulative effects of differential assignments:

> My office mate was a white male and it was quite interesting to me to see how he interacted with the person he was assigned to, how he spoke to her about the types of work assignments he was getting. It was an eye-opening experience. I learned that people don't just take assignments that are given, there's a whole lot

of back and forth and give and take. Minority women, generally, would acquiesce and want to be helpful and accommodating. They would take any work assignment that came their way, which made them prone to get work assignments with difficult partners, difficult clients, the less interesting work, or work that was not particularly relevant or involved. They would help out on a deal as opposed to running the deal. . . . I think a lot of minorities come into a situation and want to do well and get the "A" and maybe don't think as strategically as some of our counterparts. I think that is particularly noticeable in the early years as you start to develop. After a few years, it's a self-fulfilling prophecy because then they can say, "Hey, this person has had much more responsibility with the client, they have a client relationship and done lots of different types of deals, and this other person hasn't really gained the same level of responsibility." But that's directly related to the opportunities they were given.

The cumulative effect of dead-end and uninspiring assignments led one woman of color to look elsewhere for professional fulfillment:

I have not had a lot of opportunities for professional development. Junior minority associates, especially females, are required to do a lot of document review, whereas our white male counterparts do more challenging assignments and a lot more writing. When I am given writing or research assignments, the assignments are usually short-term emergencies which do not create learning or development. That is why I am leaving my firm for a federal clerkship and I highly doubt I will ever return.

In sum, 44% of all women of color reported missing out on desirable assignments compared to only 2% of white men. They were more likely than their white male counterparts to get stuck in dead-end or undesirable assignments early in their careers while their white male colleagues were assigned higher-level work and given exposure to clients. Many women of color wanted to influence which assignments were given to them and see less subjectivity in the allocation of assignments. Some women of color were unaware that

assignments could be negotiated; those who did found ways to avoid getting stuck in dead-end assignments, and got assigned instead to higher-level work. Over time, as white male colleagues received increasingly challenging assignments, real differences began to emerge in the experience and skill levels of women of color and their white male counterparts, resulting in a momentum that benefited the careers of white male attorneys and hindered the careers of women of color.

Specialization

A white woman attorney in the survey wrote, "Like many other women in the early to mid-1980s, I was tracked out of mainstream practice areas—corporate, litigation, securities. It is only fairly recently that women are not steered toward peripheral practice areas such as employee benefits, public finance, or estate planning."

Greater numbers of women today may work in litigation and areas of law previously denied to them and to persons of color, but social pressures to work in areas that "fit" their presumed qualities and interests persist. This was especially true for Native American attorneys in the focus groups. As one Native woman said, "People who are Native practice Indian law as opposed to other minority groups who go on to practice in a variety of legal areas."

While some women attorneys may have been content to work in areas of law with a large percentage of women, many women in the focus groups were unhappy about being tracked into some specialties and away from others. They were either not practicing in areas of law that interested them or felt they had to struggle to do so. As one woman of color explained, "I was denied opportunities to litigate in the medical malpractice section initially; I was pressured to do family law and insurance defense." An African-American woman wrote, "I wasn't able to develop a business practice despite having an MBA because the firm thought I should be a litigator due to my aggressive behavior. The business work was reserved for the male associates and some partners didn't want to work with black associates." Another African-American woman commented, "There were practice areas that were maybe higher quality or of more interest to me, such as pharmaceutical litigation, [but] the people who were assigned to those areas were either young white males or very young attractive white females."

Some women of color had doubts about reaching their career goals. One woman attorney said, "As an African-American, I am concerned that if I would like to advance in my particular area of practice—estate planning—I will be at a disadvantage, since much of the business development in this area comes from having social contacts and, for example, belonging to the right country club and summering in the Hamptons."

Incompatibilities between women's interests and legal specialties that were open to them led some women of color to leave law firms. One woman of color reported:

> My gender prevented me from getting IP (Intellectual Property) work because the partner who brings in that kind of work and distributes it prefers not to work with women—he thinks they get married and/or pregnant and leave, so why invest in them. That is why I am leaving this employer.

Firms that seek to retain women associates of color would do well to ensure that they have opportunities to enter practice areas that appeal to them.

Perceptions of Competence

Many women of color in the survey found that they had to disprove preconceived negative notions about their legal skills when they joined the firm as well as later in their careers. An African-American woman described her experience:

> I was a lateral hire and I'd had significant experience as a trial litigator. They sent the partner, who was a judge, to interview the judges before whom I had tried cases, and they'd never done that with any other person that they'd hired. Black, white, men, women. The judges before whom I had tried cases came back and told me. They still put me through the ropes. It took another year before they gave me a trial, and I had more trial experience than anybody in the firm [of more than 200 attorneys]!

Attorneys in the survey were asked to select traits and skills that they thought others attributed to them in ways that affected their careers.[1] *Women of color in the survey reported that they were perceived less favorably than their counterparts in almost every category* (see Table 2). This is vastly different from white males who, *in every category*, thought that others perceived them favorably. Given the dearth of negative career experiences reported by white men in the survey in

---

1.   Attorneys were asked how they *thought they were perceived*, not how they perceived themselves or how they actually were perceived by others.

Table 2: Attorney Perceptions of Traits Attributed to Them

Do you think you are perceived by others as having . . .	Women of color	Men of color	White women	White men
Good interpersonal communication skills	79%	84%	85%	92%
Good client relationship skills	62%	74%	85%	88%
Good technical skills	58%	72%	83%	90%
Good management skills	37%	41%	53%	60%
Good research skills	68%	61%	68%	75%
Good writing skills	74%	71%	87%	88%
Committed to career	34%	57%	58%	68%
Takes initiative	59%	70%	71%	81%
Risk taking	14%	21%	23%	37%
Good time management	39%	41%	54%	54%
Good verbal skills	65%	82%	82%	87%
Good professional appearance	57%	68%	62%	68%
Passive	1%	3%	0%	3%
Aggressive	13%	16%	18%	22%

terms of networking, assignments, mentoring experiences, performance evaluations and client contact, their perceptions that others attributed so many positive traits to them should come as no surprise. One woman of color in the survey wrote, "White colleagues generally have more credibility with partners, are more respected as smart and capable; it is assumed that they are good attorneys. As a woman of color in a conservative environment, establishing and maintaining credibility is an uphill battle."

Relatively few attorneys in the survey thought they were perceived as aggressive in a way that affected their career. Aggressiveness was more of an issue to women of color in the focus groups who reported that they tended to be seen either as less aggressive than they needed to be or as overly aggressive. Asian women in particular talked about others' skepticism about whether they could advocate aggressively for clients. An accomplished Asian attorney, a lateral hire, described her experience during interviews with prospective law firms:

Several times during interviews I was asked whether I could "aggressively" advocate for my client. This question always baffled me because I didn't consider myself to be a wallflower and yet I was perceived as being meek, despite my court and trial experience as an employment law litigator. Perhaps it was my inscrutable Asianness coming out.

Another Asian attorney explained:

I am frequently perceived as being very demure and passive and quiet, even though I rarely fit any of those categories. When I successfully overcome those misperceptions, I am often thrown into the "dragon lady" category. It is almost impossible to be perceived as a balanced and appropriately aggressive lawyer.

A Latina described her frustration with others' perceptions:

Women have to walk a careful line because it's still very easy for people to say, "Oh my God, she's a bitch, she's so hard to deal with. She pushes back so much. And once you're [labeled as] a bitch no one wants to work with you. . . . It's really hard for a woman to ask for what she

should be able to ask for and not be perceived as a bitch.

A woman of color who decided to leave her firm reported:

My white male boss called me a "bitch" in front of the entire office. He thought he was complimenting me on being tough, hardnosed and nononsense. However, I was highly offended and deeply hurt by the comment. Even though I know that the root of the comment was meant to be complimentary, it stung a lot. . . . I otherwise had very high opinions of my boss and present law firm.

Several women of color in the focus groups sensed that senior attorneys were skeptical about whether they "belonged" in the firm and that their suspicions surfaced in their low tolerance for mistakes. One woman of color said:

There is an unconscious expectation that minority associates don't really belong in the firm, so any mistake by a minority associate, a mistake commonly made by most or all associates as they learn the practice, is seen as confirmation that we didn't deserve to be there, instead of being seen as a natural part of the learning process.

An African-American woman echoed these sentiments: "White associates are not expected to be perfect. Black associates . . . have one chance and if you mess up that chance, look out. There is no room for error. Who's perfect coming out of law school?" Another woman of color said, "White males and females are given a chance to make mistakes and are coached on how to correct them. My mistakes are deemed 'monumental' and aren't told to me discreetly." An Asian-American woman who felt battered by criticism told this story:

When I was an associate, there were yellers everywhere and you got a new hole ripped if you made a mistake. I was talking to my mother and said that I understand why lawyers drink because every night I come home and I'm tense and can't sleep. My mother said, "You have no problem fighting us! When we say you did something and you disagree, you battle with us. These people are not your parents. Why are you so afraid to stand up for yourself?"

Presumed competencies worked to the advantage of women of color only when firms relied on their race or ethnicity for business purposes. As a Native woman explained:

> They were very clear about what they wanted in terms of building a practice, how much was I going to bring in and what the time frames were. I came in on a partnership track, senior counsel, so I knew what I was getting into and I've been treated very well. Marketing budgets—anything I've wanted I've had the full support of the firm. Our Indian law practice is like the jewel in our firm. We're not the step-child; we're the highest yield in collections.

An African-American woman reported that the stereotype of "the angry Black woman" worked to her advantage in getting assignments as a trial attorney:

> [They] expect a Black woman to be extremely aggressive and to do really well on trial. If you're aggressive, you're going to do well. You're going to get more money. . . . [In] my situation, its "She's going to be a tough one. She's going to get it done so give her the trial, give her the assignment. She'll be able to handle it." And hopefully it will continue.

Sometimes others presumed that women of color had skills or interests that they did not, in fact, possess. A Latina explained:

> Because I am Hispanic, people assume I speak Spanish fluently and I don't. I've been assigned document review of Spanish documents. After I've said 100 times, "No, really, I understand it but I'm not completely fluent and I'm not comfortable looking at documents," [and they reply] "Oh you'll be fine, look it up in a dictionary." People assume I'm going to be interested in a certain subject because it has to do with Latin America. You're battling a lot of stereo-

types or assumptions. And even sometimes when you push back—because I do, I don't hesitate—it's like they don't hear you sometimes.

In sum, most women of color in the survey did not think that they were perceived as favorably by others as their white and male counterparts. This was as true of more accomplished, senior-level women of color as it was of younger, less experienced associates. It is not surprising that white men considered themselves more highly regarded; their experience was not tainted by feeling marginalized and isolated, getting stuck in low-level assignments, being denied opportunities to develop client relationships, and being judged more harshly for their mistakes. The only time women of color in the study thought others presumed that they were competent was in areas in which their race was an asset with a specific clientele or in a specific situation.

Performance Evaluation

Close to one-third of women of color in the survey (31%) said that they have had at least one unfair performance evaluation, as did 25% of white women and 21% of men of color. *Less than 1% of white men reported ever having received an unfair performance evaluation.* Twenty percent of women of color reported being denied advancement or promotional opportunities, as did 27% of white women and 19% of men of color. *Only 1% of white men reported being denied advancement or promotional opportunities.* These are striking differences with major implications for how women of color gauge their career prospects relative to their counterparts, especially those of white men.

Some women of color in the survey reported that they were treated with kid gloves during their performance evaluations. This proved to be a career liability because it kept them from learning how to improve performance and advance their careers. A Native woman said, "They're afraid of hurting your feelings. I felt I needed more constructive criticism than I was getting. I felt that because I am a woman they weren't being as constructive about what I needed to do to develop further. I talked to some of the guys in the overall practice and they got more constructive criticism." An African-American woman described how "soft evaluations" damage careers:

They don't want to scare the poor minority attorneys so they give them very soft evaluations the first couple of years. They say, "Everybody likes you, you're doing well." It becomes more substantive at a mid level and they're making decisions about you and people begin to see that your skills aren't what they are supposed to be, but you didn't know because no one ever told you. It's insidious. Nobody wants to say anything negative because you have to work with that person. But eventually they'll get around to it. And people have gotten blindsided by soft evaluations, and subsequently they don't have skills that partners think they should have.

Some women of color were discouraged when their achievements were devalued relative to those of their colleagues. One woman of color recalled:

While working as an associate in a majority-owned firm, I got a very high-profile case dismissed with prejudice by the plaintiff (we represented the defendant), and I received no recognition for my accomplishment. When a white female associate won an oral argument against a pro se plaintiff, the firm announced the win to everyone by e-mail and took everyone out for drinks after work to celebrate. Her case was worth about $5,000 and my case was valued at about $1.5 million.

Women of color in the study hesitated to complain about performance evaluations. An African-American woman said:

Complaining never gets you anywhere and you certainly don't want to become bitter, so you acquiesce somewhat. You don't want to be seen as difficult so you don't refuse assignments, you don't say I'm not dealing with this person or whatever, because then you're [perceived as] not being a team player, you're [perceived as] not motivated, angry. It's always some other reason; it's never because "I'm uncomfortable working with a black woman." No one is ever going to say that.

Most women of color were prepared for frank appraisals of their work, as was the woman who said, "I don't think any young attorney wants [to be treated with kid gloves]. We just want opportunities to succeed, like everyone else." However, some women of color thought they would never be "just like everyone else." One woman attorney of color said, "When it comes down to choosing between two people who are of equal work product in everything else, that's when race plays a part. That's when you start hearing comments like, 'I just didn't like him for some reason' and 'It wasn't a good fit.'" Women of color were very conscious of subjectivity in performance evaluations and promotions, more so than their counterparts. Forty-seven percent of women of color in the survey felt strongly that evaluation processes in law firms should be less subjective, as did 30% of men of color, 31% of white women, and 13% of white men. Thirty-eight percent of women of color felt strongly that promotion processes should be less subjective, as did 26% of both men of color and white women and 10% of white men.

Salary Disparity

Salary was as important to women attorneys of color in the survey as it was to their peers. As one woman of color put it, "I'm not in it for grins." Seventy-one percent of women attorneys of color in the survey who worked in law firms were the sole breadwinner in their household, second only to white men (81%). Sixty-four percent of men of color and 61% of white women in law firms were the sole breadwinner in their households. An African-American woman attorney reported:

Throughout my career I have made it a point to let the partners know that I am the primary supporter of my family, and that has had a positive effect on my career. There were three women, including myself, who were vying for a partnership position. One of the women left of her own accord and then the partners chose

> Some women of color were discouraged when their achievements were devalued relative to those of their colleagues.

me over the other woman. One of the partners I'm particularly close to told me that he was comfortable having the other woman go and look for new opportunities because she was single, until recently, whereas I'm the sole support of my family.

The women of color in the survey reported that in 2003 their gross salary (including bonuses), on average, was $157,290. Men of color earned approximately one-third more, $210,569. White women earned two-thirds more than women of color, $254,746; white men were paid nearly double, $314,416.

Taken at face value, there appears to be a gross inequality between the salaries earned by women of color and those earned by all other attorneys. However, much of the difference in salaries could be attributed to differences between groups of attorneys in the number of years of practice, graduating from a top-tier law school, class rank at graduation from law school, firm size, initial negotiated salary, and meeting required billable hours. The statistical analysis of salary differences, conducted by NORC, revealed the following:[2]

- Salary differences existed between women and men and between white attorneys and attorneys of color *in their first decade* of practicing law, but were not statistically significant. Women of color, on average, earned $122,185, white women earned $123,129, and white men earned $134,912. Interestingly, men of color had the lowest average salary, $119,440.
- Salary differences also existed between attorneys with *20 or more years' experience* practicing law, but again, were not statistically significant. Women of color, on average, earned $359,750. White women earned, on average, $387,951 and white men $376,809. Once again, men of color reported the lowest average salary, $262,619 (73% as much as women of color).

2. Statistical significance is a statement about probabilities; specifically, the likelihood that an observed difference could have occurred by chance—technically speaking, by random error. In this example, once the number of years of practice was taken into account salary differences were too small to be statistically significant. In statistical terms the differences were too small to reject the null hypothesis of no difference.

- Women who worked for larger firms, regardless of race, reported significantly higher earnings than those at smaller firms, but the same was not true for men.
- The returns for experience were greater for women of color than for any other group. Women of color had a 6% salary increase for each additional year of work experience, while white men increased their salaries by only 2%. This could be because they began at lower salaries and with each year of experience got closer to the salaries of their white counterparts.
- Graduation from a top-tier law school increased the earnings of white men and women of color (by 23% and 17%, respectively), but had no significant impact on the earnings of white women or men of color.
- White men experienced the greatest salary benefit from a high class rank at graduation from law school (including Law Review), a gain of 22%, whereas the benefit to women of color was only 6%.
- Initial negotiated salary was the most important determinant of earnings for white men, increasing subsequent earnings by 36%. Initial negotiated salary was not a significant factor in the salaries for any of the other groups.

Nearly one in four white male attorneys (23%) negotiated their initial salary, a much higher percentage than the 6% of women attorneys of color, 16% of men attorneys of color and 13% of white women. However, such negotiation was the exception, not the rule. Eighty-seven percent of women of color, 79% of men of color, 80% of white women, and 69% of white men did not think negotiation was possible.

Attorneys who participated in the survey were asked to choose two actions that had the greatest impact on increasing their overall compensation (salary, benefits, and bonus). Fifty-two percent of white men indicated that developing a book of clients had the greatest impact on their compensation, and 31% indicated that professional or public recognition had the greatest impact. Twenty-six percent thought that staying with the same employer and 23% thought changing employers had the most important impact on increasing their overall compensation.

Women of color had different perceptions. The largest percentage of women of color in the survey indicated that changing employers (41%) had the greatest impact on their overall compensation; the second largest percentage chose staying with the same employer (28%). (The statistical analysis of salary differences revealed that changing employers had a negative impact on women's salaries; each additional employer, on average, reduced the earnings of white women by 9% and by 8% for women of color. Changing employers did not have a negative impact on men's salaries irrespective of race.)

Twenty-two percent of women of color thought that acquiring legal skills had the greatest impact and 16% thought that expanding their network inside the law firm had the greatest impact on increasing their overall compensation. Only 8% of women of color thought developing a book of clients had a significant bearing on overall compensation.

Thirty-eight percent of men of color thought changing employers and 34% thought developing a book of clients had the greatest impact on their compensation. Twenty-four percent thought that professional or public recognition had the most significant impact on compensation, and 21% said moving from the public to the private sector had the greatest effect. Among white women, 38% thought changing employers and 34% thought developing a book of clients had the greatest impact on increasing their overall compensation. However, approximately 25% of white women attorneys indicated that professional or public recognition, staying with the same employer, and expanding their internal firm network had the greatest impact on their overall compensation.

Clearly, white men, most of whom in this sample were senior to women of color, understood that developing a book of clients is a fact of life in law firms, a requirement for increasing overall compensation. Their exclusion from strategic networks and assignments that led to meaningful client contact most likely kept many women of color from indicating that developing a book of clients helped to increase their overall compensation, and led a substantial percentage to try instead to maximize compensation through lateral moves. Ironically, lateral moves depressed rather than increased their overall compensation—except, perhaps, for women of color

who moved from smaller to larger, better-paying law firms.

Billable Hours

The pressure to meet billable hours weighs heavily on associates and, increasingly, on partners as well. The ABA Commission on Billable Hours Report, published in 2002, recommended that firms require attorneys to work 1,900 hours per year. The associates in the sample reported that their firms required, on average, between 1,800 and 1,900 hours.

Fewer than half of women attorneys of color (46%) said that they were able to meet billing requirements, compared to 53% of men of color, 59% of white women, and 58% of white men. Whether this reflects an insufficient client base, lack of assignments from partners in the firm, difficulty balancing demands of work and family, or some other reason cannot be ascertained from this study. Some women of color reported that they were asked to do a disproportionate amount of non-billable, firm-related work such as writing articles for partners, editing partners' books, etc., and that these projects kept them from meeting required billable hours. One woman of color made this observation about billable hours and work assignments:

> It is widely known among associates at my firm that men receive more challenging and dynamic assignments than the women attorneys. It is my perception, based on informally interviewing my colleagues, that the female minority attorneys receive the "last choice" work assignments. Since the assignment of substantive work to attorneys directly relates to their ability to bill— the bottom line—the result of poor work assignments becomes cyclical, making it difficult for me (or others like me) to meet the billable-hour requirement and develop my skill set.

Some women attorneys of color felt career rewards were not forthcoming even when they met billable-hour requirements and brought in business early in their career. A Native woman explained:

> Partnership is based partially on bringing in money and business. I understand that you also

have to build your legal skills. I asked [the partners at my firm], "Can I make partner sooner if I bring in more clients?" They told me no, you're not up for partner until your seventh year. My billable rate is going to be off the chart for a second-year associate, but it's not going to help me make partner any quicker.

Very few women of color in the focus groups spoke about salary inequities, except for the detrimental impact that marriage and children had on salary. One exception was a Native woman attorney who had this reaction to pay equity in her firm:

We have a pretty formal [procedure]. I'm up for equity partner this year and [I paid close attention to] a presentation in the firm on salary, particularly the numbers on equity partners [which indicated what the lowest compensation would be for the average number of billable hours]. I looked at those numbers and thought, "Good God, I bill way more than that and I make way less than the minimum. What is wrong with this picture?" It really [******] me off. And it got me to wondering where I stand in terms of compensation, if it's a racial issue.

The ability (or inability) to meet required billable hours was not a critical factor in whether women of color stayed in or left the milieu of the private law firm. Of the women of color who were able to meet billing requirements, 46% remained in law firms and 46% left. When asked about changes they would most like law firms to make, 44% of women of color, 36% of white women, 28% of men of color, and 20% of white men wanted lower billable-hour requirements.

Job Satisfaction and Mobility: The Decision to Stay or Leave

Attorneys in the survey were asked, on a scale from one to five, to rate their satisfaction with having chosen law as a profession. If their average rankings were expressed as grades, white men would have given their career satisfaction an A, white women and men of color a B, and women of color a B- or C+. These ratings were similar to attorneys' retention rates in law firms. Most white men and white women in the survey who

had worked in law firms stayed in that milieu (72% and 67%, respectively). The retention rate for women attorneys of color was 53% and for men of color, 52%. The differences in retention rates between women of color and white men and women may be due in part to generational differences; most women of color in the survey were relatively young and still in the ascendancy of their careers, prime candidates for lateral moves to maximize advancement, while most white women and white men were in the middle to late stages of their careers.[3]

Among attorneys in the survey who left private law firms, nearly half (47%) of white men became partners or shareholders in smaller law firms of fewer than 25 attorneys. Their second and third most common career moves were in-house corporate counsel (19%) and associate or of counsel in a smaller firm (12%).

Most women of color, men of color, and white women in the survey who left law firms became in-house attorneys in a corporate legal department (31%, 33%, and 36%, respectively). The second most common career move for women of color was a government position (including the Department of Justice) or a judicial clerkship (23%). The second most common career move among men of color and white women was becoming a partner or shareholder in a smaller law firm of fewer than 25 attorneys (27% of both groups). The third most common career move for women of color and white women was a job outside the legal profession (15%). (Only 9% of white men left to pursue a job outside the legal profession, the same percentage that went to work for the government.) The third most common career move for men of color was joining a firm of fewer than 25 attorneys as an associate or of counsel (14%).

By the time they left large firms, most women of color were disillusioned with the milieu; they found

---

3. It is worth noting that the retention rate for women of color in law firms in this study is inflated relative to the population of women attorneys of color in the United States. In the NALP study cited earlier in this report, 81% of minority female associates had left private law firms within five years of being hired and nearly 100% had left after eight years. The women of color in this survey were younger, had practiced law for fewer years, and had spent fewer years in law firms on average than the total population of women attorneys of color. They had yet to reach the critical "up or out" point where they were made partner or had to leave the firm.

such firms alienating, stifling, and unsupportive. Fourteen percent of women of color who left law firms stated that their primary reason for leaving was to avoid barriers to professional advancement in the organization not related to skills, competence or experience. One woman of color wrote:

> At a large law firm, I was ignored and marginalized. I was rarely challenged, despite requests to be. I felt stifled and frustrated, not to mention exhausted and bored. I could not relate to the partners who seemed more focused on money and material things rather than life and happiness. I was often not included in meetings and no one really knew me or what I was capable of doing.

An African-American woman said, "Even though my assignments were good, my relationship with the partners was nonexistent. I felt like I lived in a completely different universe. So even though I had great assignments and things went well on the outside, I felt incredibly lonely and isolated at the firm. I always felt as though I did not belong." Another woman of color described her experience:

> I left the law firm for a variety of reasons. A major reason that I was not valued at the firm, I believe, [was] because of my gender and race. I worked long hours on several high-profile cases and successfully litigated two pro bono cases, but I was not valued by the senior attorneys. There were very few partners and senior associates of color. The only Black partner and several mid-level minority associates left the firm during my time there. As a minority associate there were very few opportunities for advancement, because most of the desirable cases were reserved for the favored associates who were mostly male and white. Nepotism was looked upon favorably at the firm, and [sexual] relationships between partners and associates were acceptable to many. In sum, I never felt I fit in because of the "boys' club" mentality of the leadership and cliquish behavior of the lawyers.

The absence of attorneys of color at the partnership level was especially disheartening to women associates of color. One woman of color wrote, "If a high percentage of women and minorities are stuck at the senior associate rank for no obvious reason, this causes the third- through sixth-year associates to believe that advancement is impossible, so they leave." A Latina explained, "I think minorities and women lateral out of the large law firms to go to places with a more reasonable life/work balance. . . . Most minorities end up in-house or out of law. I don't think they stay at firms. Which means no one is ever going to get to the top level to help fix the bottom."

A few women of color in the focus groups reported that the culture of their law firm clashed with their cultural or religious practices. An Asian woman recalled an incident with her mentor: "[She told me] over a fancy lunch that I should give up being a vegetarian if I wanted to get ahead and be successful with clients who want to work with someone who can order them a steak. I explained that I could not do this because of my religion, Hinduism, but she dismissed that curtly."

Although moving from a large firm to a small firm was uncommon among women of color, those who did so were more comfortable there. They no longer felt alienated from other attorneys, they felt the environment was friendlier and more informal, and allowed them greater flexibility in balancing the demands of family and personal life. They also reported getting more career-building assignments. A woman of color in the survey wrote, "I have nothing positive to say about large private firms. I am now at a smaller firm (40 attorneys) and I'm much more content. They can't let you fall through the cracks or give you bogus nonessential assignments that neither showcase your talents nor challenge your skills." Another woman of color commented, "In a smaller firm, at least the one I was in, they tried very hard to incorporate everyone." An African-American woman echoed these sentiments:

> I went to a smaller firm of about 30 lawyers where I was the only African-American lawyer

Fourteen percent of women of color who left law firms stated that their primary reason for leaving was to avoid barriers to professional advancement in the organization not related to skills, competence or experience.

but, strangely enough, I felt more comfortable. There were a number of very strong and positive female role models there, both partners and senior associates, and women who were getting great assignments and were seen as being on the partnership track.

One woman of color pointed out that smaller departments within large law firms could be as sustaining and career-enhancing as life in a smaller firm. As she explained:

During most of my career, I have worked either in a smaller law firm (under 50 lawyers) or in a small and specialized group within a large firm (500+ lawyers). As a result, I have always had opportunities to do good-quality, high-profile work and to develop close mentoring and working relationships with partners and other senior lawyers. It is my impression that women of color who work in the larger, more generalized practice groups of the firms where I have worked—for example, litigation, mergers and acquisitions—have had fewer such opportunities.

Not all women of color were enamored with smaller firms. One woman of color said, "In a larger firm it's easy to get lost in the shuffle, but you also have a bigger pool of partners that you can choose from." Another felt protected by the formal personnel rules of larger firms. She wrote:

To be honest, I have had less difficulty being a woman of color in a larger firm environment than in a smaller firm. In a larger firm there are processes set up whereby I felt protected, and in the event that I felt threatened or disadvantaged (which was not often) those actions would not be tolerated. In a large-firm environment there is less room for such behavior. In a smaller firm, there are really no processes in place. They are run like a sole proprietorship and people get away with more.

When moving from their law firm to a subsequent position, most attorneys in the survey relied on family, friends, and business associates, irrespective of race or gender. However, only 13% of women of color used

business associates to find subsequent positions, compared to 24% of white men, 25% of white women, and 22% of men of color. It may be that women of color did not need business associates to find their next position, but it may also be that limited opportunities to develop business relationships precluded using them in their job search.

Of course, retention is not a one-way street; law firms can choose to terminate employees. Several attorneys of color in the focus groups felt that termination processes were tinged with racial or gender biases and were not meritocratic. A Latina said, "As soon as the market crashed [in the 1990s], the first people to go were people of color. What made it even more ridiculous to some of us was that we had much higher credentials than the white males who were being hired." Another Latina observed:

When the [attorneys of color] left they were all made to feel like they were incompetent, like they didn't know what they were doing, and they didn't have the credentials to be there. But when I think about everyone who left, they all went on to become general counsels of corporations—big corporations—and they're all very successful.

A woman of color described her experience:

In 1995, I was promoted to counsel, along with three white male colleagues. Each was made partner in the succeeding years, except for me. The firm has never made an African-American woman partner. I generally get scraps of work as opposed to the real assignments. I have stayed because of the money and the fact that I have the freedom to pursue interests outside of the firm. Eventually I will change careers.

Some law firms were at a loss about how to attract and retain women attorneys of color. One white attorney in the survey wrote that it was very difficult to find attorneys of color with the skills his firm was looking for, and when they found them they could not keep them. Sometimes women of color went to a different firm; sometimes they left to work for a corporation that offered similar compensation and a larger array of benefits, and a better quality of life. Another white male attorney wrote that retention rates would improve if the pool of candidates were greater so that competition between firms for women of color would not be so intense. A third white male attorney candidly explained, "We never achieved an appropriate level of making this associate [who was a woman of color] feel included."

Marriage and Family

Many white women and women of color in the study recognized the incompatibility between the demands of a career in a private law firm and their personal life. A Latina explained, "The women that I know who have made partner and who are at the top echelons of the corporate environment are either not married, or they're married with no children, or their husbands stay home and take care of the kids. So that's not a great story for women, by and large." A Native American woman reported that in her firm, "All the female partners waited to have children until after they made partner—the female partner who had children while she was an associate had to take a year extra to make partner." An African-American woman said, "I'd like to have a family, I'd like to have relationships outside of work and it doesn't seem like it's something that even the most talented women partners were able to manage. So I'm not going to stay and try to achieve that and then find myself miserable with what I've got." A Latina described her dilemma:

I have been working with and have been mentored by a very senior white male partner and it's been great. And I'm still a flight risk. Part of the reason I stopped actively looking somewhere else was that I really did feel like he was investing in me. . . . But in terms of being there at the top to carry on his legacy, I mean . . . the chances are so slim. I got what I wanted and found at the end of the day it probably won't be enough; I'll probably want to take some time with my kids . . . . I'm not going to be the very aggressive supermom, working 18 hours a day until I make capital partner. That's the model I see at my firm, and I know that that's not me.

Another woman of color said:

The law firm "system" is not designed to accommodate professionals with complex lives,

various professional/civic interests, or differing opinions on the importance of work in their lives overall. This reality negatively impacts women of color in particular because our lives tend to be more complicated due to care-giving responsibilities and strong commitments to non-professional pursuits.

Some of the focus group participants saw marriage as a career liability for women but not for men. An African-American woman attorney explained:

The male associates all had stay-at-home wives who took care of all the everyday things. So even if they didn't have children, their dry cleaning was picked up, their dinner was cooked, their house was cleaned. And women have to do all that stuff on top of their work.

Another woman of color said:

I am single and I have to do everything for myself. I work primarily with white men who are married. They view my marital status as a benefit; it allows me to work without feeling bad about neglecting anyone. What they don't understand is that I don't have the opportunity to form close relationships, and that's hard.

Some women of color felt forced to choose between the "motherhood track" and the "partnership track"; some had the choice made for them. Some had cases taken away because they were pregnant; some were considered less committed to their careers when they expressed an interest in starting a family. One woman of color said, "They think that if you're a working mother you're not totally committed. For me, that's a bigger problem than being a minority." A Native woman attorney with an eye on the bottom line explained, "As a partner, you have to pull your fair share regardless of what's going on. If you want more time for your family, I think they would be more than happy to make you of counsel, but they're not going to want you to get the same benefits [based on what you're each] billing."

When asked if others questioned their career commitment after they gave birth or adopted a child, *72% of women of color and white women said yes, as did only 15% of men of color and 9% of white men.* (Bear in mind that almost three-quarters of women of color and 61% of white women are the primary or sole bread-winners in their household.) A white woman lawyer wrote, "Married women are assumed not to need the money and, therefore, the client business and senior leadership spots."

Thirteen percent of men of color and 4% of white men reported that others perceived them as being *even more* committed to their careers when they became a parent; only 2% of women of color and none of the white women thought they were perceived this way. A white woman attorney in the survey wrote, "When men need time off to handle family matters, people think it reflects well on them. When women need time off to handle family matters, it is seen as a lack of commit-ment or a weakness."

A Native American woman described a woman at her firm, a well-liked and highly regarded litigator, who had children and came back to work part-time, but who left the firm because she could not meet travel demands.

> Native American attorneys gave particularly poignant descriptions of the clash between the demands of the law firm and family.

An Asian woman partner de-scribed the comments she re-ceived about work/family trade-offs: "I get that a lot: 'Don't you feel bad leaving your kids at home? Don't you miss them?' And I say 'Sure, I miss them. My husband misses them too, but I have a won-derful relationship with my kids; my children are fabu-lous.' And they say, 'Oh, my wife could never do that, never leave the kids.'" An-other Asian woman said, "The problem I see is that they really don't understand what you're doing here. They may prize you as a lawyer, they may think you're a heck of a litigator, but deep down they're wondering, 'What's she doing here? Why isn't she home with the kids like my wife is?' It's a real problem when people just don't get what you do."

Native American attorneys gave particularly poi-gnant descriptions of the clash between the demands of the law firm and family. One woman described her unease when she traveled home for non-Christian holi-days to visit her family:

I was the first in my family to graduate high school and college and law school. . . . I have to remind people [at my firm] if I want to take leave or go home for a week, and they tell me that they don't want me to take off that week. Then I have to explain that I can't reschedule, it's for religious, cultural stuff. They're fine with it but you can sense they're thinking, "How do I know that is what is really going on? It's not on my calendar." I sometimes feel like people look at me and wonder, "Is she really going to Hawaii?"

Other Native American women felt intensely lonely living far away from their family and worried that their career would interfere with family relationships. One woman said, "I don't really have a life other than my family support system; especially for Native Ameri-cans, your extended family is so important and cen-tral." Another commented, "I'm the only person in my family who doesn't live in Alaska. It's hard to live so far away. You're away from your people and your tribe and your culture. And they think that you forget them and you're snobby."

Work/family trade-offs were real for women in this study. Unlike white men, most did not have someone at home who could take care of household and child-rearing responsibilities. Most women, regardless of color, were primary breadwinners in their households; their incomes supported their families, so work/family conflicts were professionally and financially wrench-ing. Women of color whose cultural and religious tra-ditions differed from those of mainstream lawyers and the Christian calendar also experienced work/family conflicts and worried that others questioned the legiti-macy of the time off they needed. Some women of color thought law firms should develop alternative tracks for advancement within the firm that would of-fer talented women opportunities for advancement while caring for their families; others expressed con-cerns that they would be tracked onto a career path for women only. Until law firms find a way to accommo-date the additional demands of women's lives, many women will leave law firms to work in other milieus women who otherwise would have been valuable as-sets to the firm.

Perspectives on Long-term Career Goals

Twenty-eight percent of white men in the survey ranked becoming a partner in a private law firm as one of their top two career goals, as did 19% of men of color, 17% of white women, and only 9% of women of color. The fact that white men were three times more likely than women of color to choose partnership in a law firm as a top goal is not surprising. As one woman of color wrote, "I observed that most, if not all, attorneys of color were overlooked for promotions, advances, and interesting case assignments. Most of us left upon concluding that we were not going to be considered for promotion." Women of color in the survey were excluded from professional networks and passed over by white mentors; they watched desirable assignments consistently handed to a group of attorneys of a different race or gender; they more often had only superficial contacts with clients and were denied opportunities to build meaningful relationships with them; and they found that marriage and family were career liabilities. The road to partnership for them was steeper than it was for white men and had many more hurdles and disincentives.

Less than 5% of women of color, white women and white men were interested in becoming a solo practitioner; 8% of men of color were interested in doing so. Approximately 12% of women of color, men of color and white women were interested in becoming a judge; only 8% of white men had a similar goal. Twenty percent of women of color wanted to work for a personal cause, as did 12% of white men, 11% of white women, and 9% of men of color.

Financial success was a top career goal for 32% of women of color, 36% of men of color, 24% of white women and 29% of white men. A white male attorney wrote: "I do not believe the life of a law firm is one that very many normal people would want. At this point, it is soulless, with little friendship or human kindness. I doubt many women really want to work in an institution held together primarily by greed." The soulless qualities of law firms and the lack of friendship and human kindness troubled many women of color in the survey, but none complained about the financial incentives and rewards.

Recognition of their legal expertise was also a top career goal for many lawyers in the survey. Forty-eight percent of white men, 35% of white women, 28% of men of color and 23% of women of color listed recognition of their legal expertise as one of their top two career goals.

The category most often checked by women of color was not a career goal but rather a job attribute: personal flexibility. This was a top priority for 43% of women of color, 31% of white women, 20% of men of color, and 16% of white men. Most women of color wanted to accommodate marriage and family in their lives but, as we have seen, many did not think that this was possible within private law firms. However, law firms interested in retaining women attorneys of color would do well to find ways to accommodate their need for personal flexibility given its importance to these women.

Summary and Conclusion

There was a sense among the women of color in this study that white male attorneys are the "first string" players in private law firms. They dominate the profession in general and, more specifically, the equity and managing partnerships of private firms. Race and gender may have helped women of color to get jobs with law firms interested in diversifying their staff of attorneys, but those assets evaporated once they began working at a firm. Once hired, 49% of women of color experienced demeaning comments or harassment; only 3% of white men did. Women of color in the survey and focus groups felt they could not "be themselves;" they downplayed and homogenized their gender and racial/ethnic identities. Some tried to act like the men in their firms, become "one of the boys"; others played down their femininity and tried to "mannify" themselves. The effort to minimize the impact of their physical differences was stressful to many women of color, an added burden to the long hours and hard work demanded by their firm.

Well over half of the women of color in the survey (62%) reported being excluded from informal and formal networking opportunities. They found themselves marginalized and peripheral to professional networks within the firm. They felt lonely and deprived of colleagues who would share important career-related information. Only 4% of white men felt the same way.

Women of color in the survey reported having been mentored formally and informally (43% and 83%, respectively), but many did not have mentors who ensured that they were integrated into the firm's internal networks, received desirable assignments (especially those that helped them meet required billable hours) or maintained substantive contacts with clients. Sixty-seven percent of women of color wanted more and/or better mentoring by senior attorneys and partners; only 32% of white men expressed a similar need. Women of color were less likely than any other group to have been mentored by white male attorneys. Given that the most powerful people in law firms tend to be white men and that promotion within law firms hinges in part on sponsorship by a person with power, not having a powerful white male mentor put women of color at a disadvantage relative to their white male counterparts.

> Many women of color became stuck in dead-end assignments, so that as third- and fourth-year associates, their experience lagged behind their white male counterparts, limiting their advancement potential and career trajectories.

In addition to these career hurdles, women of color in the survey and focus groups reported feeling that they had to disprove preconceived, negative notions about their legal abilities. This particularly rankled women of color who had proven track records as litigators or trial attorneys and found they had to prove themselves again after a lateral career move. Many women of color became stuck in dead-end assignments, so that as third- and fourth-year associates, their experience lagged behind their white male counterparts, limiting their advancement potential and career trajectories. Forty-four percent of women of color reported having missed out on desirable assignments—as did 2% of white men. Assignments affected their respective abilities to meet their firm's required billable hours. Forty-six percent of women of color were able to meet required billable hours—as were 58% of white men.

Forty-three percent of women of color reported having limited access to client development opportunities—as did 3% of white men. In fact, women of color found that they were brought to meetings with clients only when their race or gender or both would be advantageous to the firm; they frequently did not have a substantive role in those meetings. This prevented them from developing business contacts that they could use to develop a book of clients or as resources for finding subsequent positions.

Nearly one-third of women of color reported receiving unfair performance evaluations—as did less than 1% of white men. Sometimes their accomplishments were not acknowledged by the firm or were not as highly rewarded as those of their peers. On the other hand, many women of color felt that their mistakes were readily noted and at times exaggerated. Women of color reported being handled with kid gloves during performance evaluations and that this denied them the opportunity to correct deficits and develop strategies to gain experiences that could lead to promotions and partnership. Twenty percent of women of color reported that they were denied promotion opportunities—as did 1% of white men.

Salary was a high priority for women of color in the study. More than 70% were the sole or primary breadwinner in their household—as were 81% of white men. Though salary differences between majority and minority attorneys were not statistically significant, attorneys of color nonetheless made less money than their white counterparts. Seventy-two percent of women of color thought others perceived them as less committed to their careers after bearing (or adopting) children—so did 9% of white men.

The stress of second-class citizenship in law firms led many women of color to reconsider their career goals. Many left firms to work in other settings (especially corporations) that were lucrative, where they thought others' decisions about their careers would be less idiosyncratic, based more on merit, and that offered greater flexibility in balancing personal life, family, and work.

The lopsided experiences of women of color and white men were ultimately reflected in very different retention rates. The retention rate for women of color in law firms in this study was 53%; the retention rate for white men was 72%.

In many respects, the careers of white women attorneys and men attorneys of color were not as disadvantaged as those of women attorneys of color nor as privileged as those of white men. A lower percentage of men attorneys of color reported experiencing discriminatory career events compared to white women, such as missing out on desirable assignments (25% and 39%, respectively), blocked access to networking opportunities (31% and 60%, respectively), limited client development opportunities (24% and 55%, respectively), blocked advancement and promotion opportunities (19% and 28%, respectively), receiving unfair performance evaluations (19% and 27%, respectively), and receiving demeaning comments or harassment (34% and 47%, respectively). Men attorneys of color and white women were more alike in terms of how they felt others judged their competencies, their desire for more and better mentors, their rates of being selected as protégés by white men and their desire to become partners in law firms. White women, on average, had higher salaries than men of color but the differences were not statistically significant. However, their retention rates were quite different: 52% of men of color and 67% of white women chose to remain in law firms.

Charlotte Ray, the first African-American woman to be admitted to the bar in the United States, would surely view women's careers in today's law firms with great consternation. She would undoubtedly empathize with their decisions to leave law firms and pursue legal careers in other milieus, an option that was unavailable to her. She would, perhaps, recommend to law firms interested in retaining women of color that they devise and implement strategies to ensure that women attorneys of color receive the professional training and resources required to succeed in that environment. This includes ensuring that after they are hired, women of color are integrated quickly into firm networks, have opportunities to do meaningful work with powerful attorneys, receive assignments that will help them meet required billable hours and develop their legal skills, enable them to specialize in areas of interest to them, help them develop substantive relationships with clients, and minimize conflicts between work and family. Charlotte Ray would, no doubt, ensure that those in power in law firms understand the unique disadvantages experienced by women attorneys of color and require that all lawyers in the firm take steps to minimize those disadvantages. Perhaps her recommendations to retain and promote women of color in law firms would parallel those developed by the ABA Commission on Women, which can be found in the following section.

Recommendations

Integrate Women of Color into Existing Diversity and Professional Development Efforts

Based on the research from the focus groups and the survey, the ABA Commission on Women proposes the following recommendations for law firms that we think will be of use in integrating women of color fully into diversity efforts. Because every firm is different, we recommend that you take the following suggestions and make them your own to ensure the greatest success. This list of suggestions is also not intended to be exclusive of other strategies that may help your firm to address these issues in a way that works best for you. We encourage you to be inclusive, creative and diligent in creating and sustaining diversity and professional development strategies that foster the successful careers of women of color.

> Before you utilize the recommendations presented below, first assess the totality of your diversity initiatives and whether women of color are integrated into those initiatives.

Before you utilize the recommendations presented below, first assess the totality of your diversity initiatives and whether women of color are integrated into those initiatives. If your firm already has a thriving diversity initiative that has been incorporated into the overall business strategic plan, make sure that women of color are fully integrated into that effort. This study clearly evidences that if women of color are not viewed as separate from women in general or people of color in general, your ability to recruit, retain and advance them is impaired. When women of color are acknowledged as a unique group with unique needs within your larger diversity and professional development efforts, you are more likely to see the kinds of successes that we all know are possible. If your firm does not already have a diversity initiative, then ensure the integration of women of color as the initiative is being developed and implemented.

NOTE: These recommendations are based on the research from the survey and focus group components of the ABA Commission on Women's Women of Color Research Initiative and are focused primarily on what law firms, as institutions, can do to increase the presence and success of women of color in their attorney ranks. We are currently finishing a supplement to this research focusing specifically on women of color who have reached notable levels of success in law firms, and we will be publishing strategies for women of color on how to succeed in law firms when this supplemental research is completed.

1. Address the Success of Women of Color as a Firm Issue

By delegating the success of women of color to women of color, law firms have not fully focused on the success of women attorneys of color as a firm issue. Many of the survey and focus group respondents in this study discussed how many firms overburdened women of color through diversity committee assignments, recruiting assignments and other such efforts that marginalize the diversity efforts and place women of color in conflicting roles that compete for limited time. If firms focused instead on the success of women of color being a firm issue, then the women of color would be less burdened with these responsibilities and the overall initiatives would have a greater chance of succeeding because it would be in everyone's best interests to succeed, not just women of color's interests.

Women of color should definitely continue to be included in a firm's diversity and professional development efforts because their voices are critical in these processes, but they should not be relegated to committees that focus on diversity, nor should they assume responsibility for the creation and maintenance of diversity within the firm. To accomplish this, firm leaders should (1) talk specifically about women of color as a category of success being measured in diversity initiatives, (2) give responsibility to practice group leaders to monitor and advance the careers of women of color in their practice areas, and (3) make sure that women of color are being groomed for leadership positions in firms the same way that their white male counterparts are. This type of leadership responsibility is especially effective when the firm's leaders take on active roles in diversity committees and assume the responsibility for the success of diversity efforts in the firm.

2. Integrate Women of Color into Existing Measurement Efforts

Integrate the measurement of successes with women of color into your overall measurement efforts, especially in areas of recruiting, retention, promotion, mentoring, professional development, and client development. For example, if you are looking at the demographic composition of your summer class, measure the number of women, men of color and women of color separately so that you can see if you are indeed achieving successes in all areas for each group.

Similarly, when you examine attrition, assignment allocation, mentoring and other key areas that ultimately affect retention and advancement of your lawyers, examine the numbers for women of color as a separate category so that you can see if your diversity efforts are working perhaps just for white women or men of color instead of comprehensively across racial and gender lines. For example, regularly monitoring both the quantity and quality of work assigned to women of color enables you to quickly assess if a woman of color may be at risk of not having the amount and kind of work she needs to be on par with her colleagues. This regular monitoring can be done by a mentor, a practice group leader or someone on the diversity committee, but it is critical that key areas of professional development such as work flow are monitored closely so that potential problems are detected and addressed before a woman of color becomes an attrition risk.

The issue of measurement is of critical importance in examining salary disparities in your firm. The structure of law firm compensation systems allows for a great degree of variability in how and what people get paid. Understanding the variability through many perspectives is critical to ensuring equal opportunity for all lawyers instead of merely assuming that the compensation system is meritocratic. Compensation reflects how the firm values each lawyer's contribution and skills; therefore, disparities in the firm's compensation system may indicate that other issues (such as staffing, mentoring, etc.) need to be addressed.

Since "what gets measured gets done," the more you include women of color in your measurement of diversity efforts, the more success you will see with women of color in your firm.

3. Integrate Women of Color into the Firm's Professional Fabric

Take definitive steps to ensure that women of color truly have equal opportunities to access the best work, client relationships, informal mentoring, committee assignments, leadership opportunities, and client development support. Without a clear and visible effort to integrate women of color into the work and roles that matter the most in a firm, "diversity efforts" will be perceived by women of color as "window dressing." A clear and visible effort may sometimes mean change, such as shifting from a purely "free market" staffing system that is dependent on personal relationships to a monitored staffing system that ensures equal opportunity for all.

For example, even if a particular woman of color is "making" her hours, a closer look at the kinds of assignments that comprise her hours can alert you to a situation where a lawyer may, in fact, not be integrating into the firm's professional fabric.

4. Integrate Women of Color into the Firm's Social Fabric

This study clearly indicates that one of the greatest challenges facing women of color in law firms is isolation in the workplace at rates far greater than those faced by white men, white women or men of color. What the study also tells us is that integration into the social fabric of a law firm is critical to understanding the critieria for success. As you think about the culture of your firm, explore ways to ensure that everyone in the firm is truly included in that culture. For example, if many of the firm's "cultural activities" have traditionally not received great attendance from women of color, solicit their opinion about activities that they would attend.

Law firm culture is, for better or worse, heavily dependent on the actions of the partners in the firm. Encourage firm partners to reach out to and include women of color in social activities, ranging from informal "hellos" in the hallways and "drop-ins" into offices to periodic lunches and invitations to client events. Actions taken by partners in the firm that include women of color will greatly decrease the isolation felt by so many women of color.

5. Increase Awareness of Issues of Women of Color through Dialogue

This study demonstrates the critical nature of race and gender issues for women of color in law firms as well as the discomfort commonly felt by white men in dealing with these issues. Recommendations 1-4 will be difficult to implement if white men, most particularly those in power, continue to face discomfort in candidly and constructively discussing these issues in the workplace. Increasing awareness about these issues across the firm through activities that promote dialogue is an important step in laying the foundation

for success. Although diversity training has conventionally been used to promote dialogue, thinking more creatively about the various ways in which true dialogue can be promoted within the firm will be more successful than depending on the artifice of "diversity training."

6. Support Women of Color's Efforts to Build Internal and External Support Systems

Given the lack of a critical mass of women of color in law firms, women of color in the firm may benefit from a formal or informal affinity group. Affinity groups are an excellent way for women of color to get together, share best practices, seek advice from each other on issues, and support each other's successes. If the law firm already has affinity groups, support the creation of an affinity group for women of color. If the firm does not have affinity groups, support the informal building of a women of color community.

In addition to internal networks, many women of color will look externally for support systems, such as women's bar associations, bar associations of color, networking groups, etc., to find camaraderie, mentoring, client development opportunities and other professional assistance that they may feel eludes them in their firms. Supporting, both financially and professionally, women of color in building these external support systems demonstrates an awareness of their critical issues and an openness to finding unique solutions to addressing unique problems.

7. Stay Compliant with Anti-discrimination and Anti-harassment Policies and Hold People Accountable for Noncompliance

Your firm probably already has rigorous policies in place governing behaviors and comments that can be perceived as racist, sexist or harassing by people in your firm. The leadership of a firm should ensure that the firm consistently complies with all of these policies. Diversity and professional development efforts aimed at creating greater opportunities for success for women of color need to start with the creation and maintenance of a workplace where women of color are not subjected to demeaning, discriminatory and unwanted comments. When a firm becomes aware of individuals who are not in compliance with these policies, promptly holding the individuals accountable for their actions is critical in communicating a message that the workplace is indeed a place where everyone is welcome.

Women of color, as reported in this study, not only are more likely to experience demeaning, discriminatory and harassing comments, but they, given their vulnerability in the workplace, are also less likely to report these behaviors. A clear focus on creating a workplace where people can indeed report these incidents and where individuals are held accountable for inappropriate behavior is a first and necessary step in creating a diverse workplace for all, especially women of color.

As indicated above, these recommendations are not exhaustive, but reflect information gathered from the research. Implementation of some or all of these recommendations will enhance the success of the women attorneys of color in your firm and the overall success of the firm as well.

Survey Cover Letters and Telephone Screening

Initial Contact E-mail Letter

[DATE, YEAR]

Dear Attorney,

Recently, the American Bar Association Commission on Women in the Profession sent you an e-mail describing a study being conducted on their behalf by National Opinion Research Center (NORC), a not-for-profit social science research organization at the University of Chicago.

At this time, we ask that you draw your attention to the attached document for the study. The full document contains a letter addressing the study's objectives and issues of confidentiality as well as the survey that we are asking you to complete. If you have questions about opening the attachment, please contact us.

To participate, please print out the survey, complete it, and return it by mail or fax.
You can return it by mail to:

NORC
Project #6255
1 North State Street
Chicago, IL 60602

Or by fax to: 312-201-4676

To alleviate the cost of doing so, we will be sending you a package via First Class mail within the next few days containing a business-reply envelope in which you may return the questionnaire if you choose not to use the methods described above.

If you have any questions or concerns about the study or NORC, please e-mail us at ABA-Research@norc. uchicago.edu or contact us directly by telephone at (312) 759-5095.

Thank you for your attention.

Sincerely,
M. Mandy Sha
Project Director
NORC, University of Chicago

Group ID#: 6255-[GROUP ID]

[FIRST NAME] [LAST NAME]
[ADDRESS 1] [ADDRESS 2]
[CITY], [STATE], [ZIP]

December, 2004

Dear Attorney,

Recently, the National Opinion Research Center (NORC) at the University of Chicago sent you an e-mail containing a questionnaire regarding a study being conducted on behalf of the ABA Commission on Women in the Profession. The study seeks to examine the experiences of attorneys in the legal profession.

Regardless of your race or gender, your experiences as a member in the legal community are relevant to this study. Specifically, the study seeks to compare the experiences of women of color attorneys and those of male and Caucasian female attorneys. To prevent this comparison from being one-sided and to achieve fair representation of all members of the legal profession, it is essential that we gather information from a diverse group.

NORC, the not-for-profit social science research organization conducting the study, employs stringent practices to ensure participants' confidentiality. Please be assured that the information you provide will be used for research and statistical purposes only. All personally identifying information is separated from your responses, and results from the survey will be reported in summary form.

We understand that you have many demands on your time. However, we hope that you will take a few minutes to contribute to this important analysis. If you have not already-done so, please complete the questionnaire attached to our earlier e-mail and return it in the business reply envelope provided with this letter. Another copy is also enclosed.

Should you have questions or concerns, please contact us at 312-759-5095 or by e-mail at ABA-Research@norc.uchicago.edu. You may find additional information about this study and NORC at http://www.norc.org/issues/statmeth.asp.

Thank you in advance for your participation.

Sincerely,

M. Mandy Sha
Project Director
NORC, University of Chicago

Group ID#: 6255-[GROUP ID]

Telephone Eligibility Screening/Follow-Up Script

Hi, this is [INTERVIEWER NAME] from NORC at the University of Chicago. I am calling to follow up about the focus group research for the ABA Commission on Women in the Profession with women of color attorneys.

I just have a few screening questions to make sure that you are eligible to participate.

1. Have you ever worked in a private law firm with 25 or more attorneys some time in your career after graduation?

   No → We are sorry, at this time the focus group is limited to attorneys who have had experience working in a private law firm. Thank you for your interest.

   Yes → Thank you.

2. We are hosting a focus group in [CITY], are you located in that city?

   No → We are sorry, at this time the focus group is limited to attorneys in [CITY]. Thank you for your interest.

   Yes → Thank you.

3. In [CITY], we are hosting the focus group with [African-American / Hispanic / Asian-American / Native American] women attorneys. Does this describe you?

   No → GO TO DOES NOT MEET REQUIREMENT IN #4

   Yes → GO TO MEETS REQUIREMENT IN #4
   Bi-Racial or Multi-Racial → (ASK) Please tell me if you also identify with additional racial/ethnic groups such as African-American, Hispanic/Latina, Asian-American, or Native American?

   Yes → GO TO MEETS REQUIREMENT IN #4

   No → GO TO DOES NOT MEET REQUIREMENT IN #4

4. **Does Not Meet Requirement** → We are sorry, at this time we are not hosting focus groups with [RACE/ETHNICITY] women attorneys in [CITY]. Thank you for your interest.

   Meets Requirement → Great. Let me now schedule a time for the focus group session with you in a minute.

   Please be advised that the focus group session will be audio-taped to make sure we have an accurate record of the information you provide and to free the moderator from constant note-taking. We will destroy all audio-tapes at the end of the study.

[ADDITIONAL PARAGRAPH TO BE READ FOR PARTICIPANTS IN SESSIONS USING WEB-STREAMING]: In your group, we will be using a web session to allow authorized NORC research staff to view the session via the Internet in Chicago. We will destroy all audio-tapes, web sessions, or DVDs at the end of the study. [READ FAQ IF NECESSARY*]

The ABA Commission on Women in the Profession will only receive a transcription of the audio-tapes without any personal identifiers. No one will know that you participated - including the ABA, Commission on Women in the Profession, and/or employer.

* FAQ FOR WEB SESSION:

NORC is using an internet service provided by "Active Group" or "Focus Vision" to transmit the focus group session using web-streaming technology. According to its Web Site (www.activegroup.net), Active Group is the pioneer and leader of live Internet broadcasting (video streaming) for Focus Groups.

Authorized NORC research staff in Chicago will be able to view the focus group through a live web session, as if they were observing in the traditional observation deck at the facility. The facility has a computer that allows transmission of images that are displayed in Microsoft Media Player on a NORC computer through broadband internet connection. The web session is secure because only NORC has the login and password to the specific focus group. Additionally, the company has agreed to NORC's Confidentiality Policy and has a security officer on site. The sessions will be recorded onto a CD after the live session. After NORC receives the CD, the service provider will destroy its copy as well as all the chat history and online events.

[ADDITIONAL PARAGRAPH TO BE READ FOR PARTICIPANTS IN THE CHICAGO SESSIONS OBSERVED BY THE RESEARCH ADVISORY BOARD]: Your group is the first focus group that we are conducting for this study on the experiences of women of color in the legal profession. Your participation not only helps represent the Latina experience in the law profession, but also helps us do our job better in the next focus groups in different cities in March and April. The members of the Research Advisory Board from the ABA Commission on Women in the Profession would like to observe your focus group session in a separate room while the session is being conducted. For those that do not live in Chicago, they will be using a web session to view the focus group via the Internet. They will not interact with you or any other participants in the focus group, nor will they interfere with the session. The only reason for their observation is to advise NORC about the way the focus group is conducted, so that we may improve our techniques. This is helpful because the facilitator is a social science researcher trained to conduct focus groups but not an attorney with all the legal expertise. As a non-profit social science research organization, we follow stringent ethical guidelines regarding the protection of your identity. We have mandated the members of the Research Advisory Board who will view the session to do the same by signing a Confidentiality and Ethics Agreement that stipulates under no circumstances will they share the information they learned in the focus group session with anyone outside the research team that would identify you in anyway. We are also happy to provide a list of members from the Research Advisory Board who will observe to you upon request. May we please have your approval?

Yes → Now, may I answer more questions or concerns that you may have?

No → Thank you.

ABA Women of Color in the Legal Profession Study

Conducted by:

NORC
A national organization for research
at the University of Chicago

Dear Attorney,

You are invited to participate in an important research study comparing experiences of women of color attorneys in private law firms with those of their peers from other backgrounds. Regardless of your race or gender, your participation is vital to the accuracy of this comparison.

The National Opinion Research Center (NORC) at the University of Chicago, a not-for-profit social science research organization, is conducting the study on behalf of the American Bar Association Commission on Women in the Profession.

We are asking for your help in completing this questionnaire. Your name was either randomly selected from the ABA Membership Database or sampled from a list of women of color attorneys who registered through the Commission's website.

Please be assured that all information you provide will be used for research and statistical purposes only, and will be held in the strictest confidence.

- Your name and contact information is only used for the purpose of administering this survey. All identifying information will be electronically separated from survey data. No one will know that you participated - including the ABA, the Commission on Women in the Profession, and/or your employer.
- We will combine your answers with the answers from all other respondents and will report the results in a summary format. No one will know your individual responses.
- Participation is voluntary. You may skip any question you do not wish to answer, but we do encourage you to take the time to answer as many questions as you can as that will add to the overall integrity of the study.

If you have questions about your rights as a participant in this research project, please call the NORC Institutional Review Board Administrator, Kathleen Parks, at (866) 309-0542.

If you have questions about this survey, please contact us by telephone at (312) 759-5095, or by e-mail at ABA-Research@norc.uchicago.edu. You may find additional information about the ABA Women of Color in the Legal Profession Study and NORC at http://www.norc.org/issues/statmeth7.asp.

Sincerely,

M. Mandy Sha
NORC Project Director

Thank you for taking the time to complete this questionnaire. Directions are provided for each question. Because not all questions will apply to everyone, you may be asked to skip certain questions.

- Please print all responses. When answering questions that require marking a box, please use an "X."
- If you need to change an answer, please make sure the old answer is completely erased or clearly crossed out.

Sponsored by

AMERICAN BAR ASSOCIATION
COMMISSION
— On —
WOMEN
— In The —
PROFESSION

Please return completed questionnaire by mail to:
NORC, Project# 6255
1 North State Street, Suite 1600
Chicago, Illinois 60602

or by fax to:
(312) 201-4676

Group ID #: 6255-100

I. Respondent Characteristics

1. **In what year did you graduate from law school?**

   □□□□ *Write in year*

2. **What was the national ranking of your law school in the year you graduated?**

   1 □ Tier 1 (Top 20)

   2 □ Tier 2 (21-40)

   3 □ Tier 3 (41 and below)

   4 □ Don't know

3. **Which of these categories best describes your class rank upon graduation?**

   1 □ Law review/Honors/Order of the Coif

   2 □ 1st quartile (not Law Review/Honors/ Order of the Coif)

   3 □ 2nd quartile (26th - 50th Percentile)

   4 □ 3rd quartile (51st - 75th Percentile)

   5 □ 4th quartile (76th - 100th Percentile)

4. **Since graduation from law school, have you ever worked as a judicial law clerk?**

   1 □ Yes

   2 □ No

5. **How many years of experience as a practicing attorney do you have?**

   □□.□ *Write in number of years*

6. **During your career as an attorney, how many different employers have you had?** *Count each firm, government agency, or corporation as a separate employer; include your present employer.*

   □□ *Write in number of employers*

7. **How many years have you worked as an attorney in a PRIVATE LAW FIRM with AT LEAST 25 ATTORNEYS?**

   □□.□ *Write in number of years*

8. **In the <u>LARGEST</u> PRIVATE LAW FIRM in which you ever worked, what was the total number of attorneys firm-wide (*all* offices)?**

   □,□□□ *Write in number of attorneys*

9. **Which of the following best describes your current employment status?**

   I am . . . *(Check one)*

   1 □ working as an associate or counsel in a PRIVATE LAW FIRM with AT LEAST 25 ATTORNEYS.

   2 □ working as a partner/shareholder in a PRIVATE LAW FIRM with AT LEAST 25 ATTORNEYS.

   3 □ working as an associate or counsel in a PRIVATE LAW FIRM with fewer than 25 attorneys.

   4 □ working as a partner/shareholder in a PRIVATE LAW FIRM with fewer than 25 attorneys.

   5 □ working as an in-house attorney in a corporate legal department.

   6 □ working as an attorney in government, including Department of Justice.

   7 □ working as an attorney in the non profit sector.

   8 □ working as a judicial clerk.

   9 □ employed but no longer practicing as an attorney.

   10 □ unemployed, retired, or otherwise out of the labor force.

   11 □ not working to stay home to raise my children.

10. **Are you the primary or sole income provider in your household?**

    1 □ Yes

    2 □ No

11. **What was your gross salary including bonuses for the calendar year 2003?**

    $□,□□□,□□□. *Write in salary*

II. Retention/Advancement vs. Attrition

IN YOUR ANSWERS TO THE QUESTIONS BELOW, PLEASE REFER SPECIFICALLY TO YOUR EXPERIENCE IN THE <u>LARGEST</u> PRIVATE LAW FIRM AT YOUR <u>HIGHEST RANKING POSITION</u> IN THAT FIRM.

12. Which of the following is the highest rank you ever held in the <u>LARGEST</u> PRIVATE LAW FIRM you ever worked for? *(Check one)*

1 ☐ Overall Firm Leadership/Executive Management (managing partner, executive committee, compensation committee)

2 ☐ Department/Group Leadership

3 ☐ Equity/Capital Partner

4 ☐ Associate

5 ☐ Of counsel

6 ☐ Staff Attorney

7 ☐ Contract attorney

8 ☐ Other *(please specify)*:

[   ]

13. How many attorneys are/were in the PRIVATE LAW FIRM (firm-wide) you refer to in question 12?

☐,☐☐☐ *Write in number of attorneys*

14. At the time you worked there, who of the following were in leadership positions (e.g. managing partner, executive committee, compensation committee, department head, etc.) at the firm you referred to in question 12? *(Check all that apply)*

1 ☐ White women

2 ☐ Women of color

3 ☐ Men of color

4 ☐ White men

15. At the time you worked at the <u>LARGEST</u> PRIVATE LAW FIRM with at least 25 attorneys, who of the following, if any, served as mentors to you within this organization? *(Check all that apply)*

		Formal program	**Informally**
a.	One or more white women	1 ☐	2 ☐
b.	One or more white men	1 ☐	2 ☐
c.	One or more men of color	1 ☐	2 ☐
d.	One or more women of color	1 ☐	2 ☐
e.	No one	1 ☐	2 ☐

16. During your legal career which of the following career changes did you make based upon your spouse's or domestic partner's career/life choices? *(Check all that apply)*

1 ☐ During my legal career I have never had a spouse or domestic partner ➔ **If no spouse or partner, go to Q17**

2 ☐ Relocated for spouse's/partner's benefit when it was not a positive career move for me

3 ☐ Took a job I really didn't want in order to be in the same location as my spouse/partner

4 ☐ Put off starting a family because spouse/partner felt it was in the interest of his/her career

5 ☐ Turned down a job/position I really wanted so spouse/partner did not have to move

6 ☐ Agreed to a "long distance" relationship so we could both have the jobs we wanted even though it meant living in different locations

17. Thinking of the <u>LARGEST</u> PRIVATE LAW FIRM in which you ever worked, approximately how many average hours (rounded to whole numbers) <u>per week</u> do/did you typically work . . .

a. as an associate (non-partner)? ☐☐☐

b. as a partner? ☐☐☐

17a. What was the average number of billing hours <u>per year</u> expected of attorneys at the law firm you described in item 17? *(If that firm did not require billing hours, enter "0" and go to question 18.)*

a. as an associate (non-partner)? ☐,☐☐☐

b. as a partner? ☐,☐☐☐

17b. On average, what percentage of that requirement did you meet?

☐☐☐%

18. In the law firm you described in item 17, was there a client development requirement?

	Yes	No
a. as an associate (non-partner)	₁☐	₂☐
b. as a partner	₁☐	₂☐

19. During your tenure at this PRIVATE LAW FIRM, what changes would you most like to have seen (or would like to see)? *(Check all that apply)*

	as an associate (non-partner)	as a partner
a. Not applicable - I was never in this category	₁☐	₂☐
b. The establishment of formal policies for reduced/alternative work arrangements	₁☐	₂☐
c. Consistent implementation of current policies relating to the workplace	₁☐	₂☐
d. Less pressure to engage in client development	₁☐	₂☐
e. Lower billable hours	₁☐	₂☐
f. More flexibility from my employer in accommodating my personal life	₁☐	₂☐
g. Greater opportunity to influence decisions on matters I worked on	₁☐	₂☐
h. Greater opportunity to shape the future direction of the office/firm	₁☐	₂☐
i. More and/or better mentoring by senior attorneys/partners	₁☐	₂☐
j. More and/or better attorney training and development	₁☐	₂☐
k. More opportunities for pro bono work	₁☐	₂☐
l. Less subjectivity in the work allocation processes	₁☐	₂☐
m. Less subjectivity in the evaluation processes	₁☐	₂☐
n. Less subjectivity in the promotion processes	₁☐	₂☐
o. More racial diversity in the work place	₁☐	₂☐
p. More gender diversity in the work place	₁☐	₂☐

20. Which of the following describes how you found your position <u>in any</u> PRIVATE LAW FIRM with at least 25 attorneys? *(Check all that apply)*

	First position	Subsequent positions in that or other firms
a. Family members/friends	₁☐	₂☐
b. Law school classmates/alumni networks	₁☐	₂☐
c. Business associates	₁☐	₂☐
d. Unsolicited resume submission to the employer	₁☐	₂☐
e. Response to an advertisement	₁☐	₂☐
f. Law school's placement office	₁☐	₂☐
g. On-campus interview process	₁☐	₂☐
h. Hired following a summer clerkship	₁☐	₂☐
i. Hired following a part-time position, or unpaid internship in that firm during law school	₁☐	₂☐
j. Recommendation of a law professor	₁☐	₂☐
k. Experience in a judicial clerkship	₁☐	₂☐

21. When accepting your <u>initial</u> position at a PRIVATE LAW FIRM with at least 25 attorneys, did you negotiate for your salary? *(Check one)*

1 ☐ I negotiated for my salary.

2 ☐ I accepted what was offered, because I did not think negotiation was possible.

3 ☐ I accepted what was offered because I elected not to negotiate, even though I believed it was an option.

22. Which of the following best describes your highest priority as a long-term career goal? *(Choose up to TWO responses)*

1. ☐ Become a partner in a PRIVATE LAW FIRM
2. ☐ Participate in law firm leadership in a PRIVATE LAW FIRM
3. ☐ Participate in leadership in an organization other than a PRIVATE LAW FIRM
4. ☐ Have my own law firm (including being a solo practitioner)
5. ☐ Hold an elected or appointed public office
6. ☐ Become a judge
7. ☐ Be/become financially very successful
8. ☐ Become recognized for my legal expertise
9. ☐ Find a job which allows for great personal flexibility
10. ☐ Work for a personal cause (e.g. environment; world peace; political candidate)
11. ☐ Have a job that allows for more leisure time

23. Envision the highest paid job you realistically expect to hold during your career. What would you estimate to be the annual earnings (salary and bonuses) paid to persons holding that job today?

$ ☐☐ , ☐☐☐ , ☐☐☐ . *Write in salary*

24. Which (if any) of the following has had a major effect on your career in PRIVATE LAW FIRMS WITH AT LEAST 25 ATTORNEYS in which you have worked? *(Check any of the following that apply)*

	Positive effect	Negative effect	Neither
a. My race	1 ☐	2 ☐	3 ☐
b. My gender	1 ☐	2 ☐	3 ☐

25. In retrospect, how satisfied are you with your choice of the law as a career? *(Check one)*

1. ☐ Very satisfied
2. ☐ Satisfied
3. ☐ Neither satisfied nor dissatisfied
4. ☐ Dissatisfied
5. ☐ Very dissatisfied

26. Please rank the following work environments from most desirable <u>for you</u> (1) to least desirable <u>for you</u> (5). *(Use each rank only once)*

a. Academic ☐

b. Corporation ☐

c. Firm ☐

d. Government ☐

e. Not-for-Profit ☐

27. In your overall experience as an attorney, which <u>two</u> of the following actions had the most important impact on increasing your overall compensation (including salary, benefits and bonus)? *(Check no more than two)*

1. ☐ Acquiring formal legal skills training
2. ☐ Acquiring additional educational credentials (e.g., LLM, MBA)
3. ☐ Changing employers
4. ☐ Moving from the public to the private sector
5. ☐ Moving from the private to the public sector
6. ☐ Staying with the same employer
7. ☐ Starting my own firm
8. ☐ Developing a book of clients
9. ☐ Expanding my internal firm network
10. ☐ Expanding my external network
11. ☐ Gaining professional or public recognition/fame

28. If the position you're referring to in this section is a former position, what was the <u>most important</u> reason for leaving? If it is a current position, what is the most important reason that you would consider leaving?
(Check one)

1 ☐ I would not consider leaving

2 ☐ To work in an organization which offers advancement opportunities my current employer does not offer

3 ☐ To avoid barriers to professional advancement in the organization not related to skills, competence, and experience

4 ☐ To change careers

5 ☐ To change geographic locations

6 ☐ To change my immediate supervisor or current supervising attorney

7 ☐ To obtain experience my current employer cannot offer

8 ☐ To return to school

9 ☐ To obtain a salary increase

10 ☐ To work for a more prestigious organization

11 ☐ To work in a more diverse workplace culture

12 ☐ To obtain greater work/life balance

13 ☐ Other *(please specify)*:

29. While working in that <u>LARGEST</u> PRIVATE LAW FIRM with at least 25 attorneys, have any of the following happened to you?
(Check all that apply)

	Based on Race	Based on Gender	In a Sexual Context
a. Experienced demeaning comments or other types of harassment	1 ☐	2 ☐	3 ☐
b. Missed out on a desirable assignment	1 ☐	2 ☐	3 ☐
c. Had a client request someone other than you to handle a matter	1 ☐	2 ☐	3 ☐
d. Experienced one or more other forms of discrimination	1 ☐	2 ☐	3 ☐
e. Experienced lack of access to informal or formal networking opportunities	1 ☐	2 ☐	3 ☐
f. Experienced lack of access to client development and client relationship opportunities	1 ☐	2 ☐	3 ☐
g. Experienced unfair performance evaluations	1 ☐	2 ☐	3 ☐
h. Been denied advancement or promotional opportunities	1 ☐	2 ☐	3 ☐

30. Were you a parent or did you become a parent (natural or adoptive), while you were working at a PRIVATE LAW FIRM of at least 25 attorneys?

1 ☐ Yes → **If yes, go to Q30a**

2 ☐ No → **If no, go to Q31**

30a. Because you had or adopted a child, were you perceived as being . . .
(Check one)

1 ☐ Very much less committed to your career

2 ☐ Somewhat less committed to your career

3 ☐ No different in how committed to your career you were

4 ☐ Somewhat more committed to your career

5 ☐ Very much more committed to your career

31. To what degree of seriousness did the <u>LARGEST</u> PRIVATE LAW FIRM employer you worked in have . . . *(Check one in each row)*

	Serious	Nominal	Non-Existent
a. Gender Initiatives?	1 ☐	2 ☐	3 ☐
b. Race/Ethnicity Initiatives?	1 ☐	2 ☐	3 ☐
c. Diversity Committee?	1 ☐	2 ☐	3 ☐
d. Diversity Coordinator/Director?	1 ☐	2 ☐	3 ☐

32. During your tenure in PRIVATE LAW FIRMS, do/did you perceive that any of the following traits/skills were attributed to you in a way that affected your career?
(Check one in each row)

	Yes, favorably	Yes, unfavorably	No	Don't Know
a. Good interpersonal communication skills	1 ☐	2 ☐	3 ☐	4 ☐
b. Good client relationship skills	1 ☐	2 ☐	3 ☐	4 ☐
c. Good technical skills	1 ☐	2 ☐	3 ☐	4 ☐
d. Good management skills	1 ☐	2 ☐	3 ☐	4 ☐
e. Good research skills	1 ☐	2 ☐	3 ☐	4 ☐
f. Good writing skills	1 ☐	2 ☐	3 ☐	4 ☐
g. Takes initiative	1 ☐	2 ☐	3 ☐	4 ☐
h. Risk taking	1 ☐	2 ☐	3 ☐	4 ☐
i. Committed to career	1 ☐	2 ☐	3 ☐	4 ☐
j. Good time management	1 ☐	2 ☐	3 ☐	4 ☐
k. Good verbal skills	1 ☐	2 ☐	3 ☐	4 ☐
l. Professional appearance	1 ☐	2 ☐	3 ☐	4 ☐
m. Passive	1 ☐	2 ☐	3 ☐	4 ☐
n. Aggressive	1 ☐	2 ☐	3 ☐	4 ☐

III. Additional Characteristics

33. In what year were you born?

☐☐☐☐ *Write in year*

34. What is your gender?

1 ☐ Male

2 ☐ Female

35. Which of the following best describes your race/ethnicity? *(Check <u>one</u>)*

1 ☐ American Indian or Alaska Native

2 ☐ Asian (origins in Far East, South or Southeast Asia)

3 ☐ Black or African American

4 ☐ Hispanic or Latino

5 ☐ Middle Eastern

6 ☐ Native Hawaiian or other Pacific Islander

7 ☐ White or Caucasian

8 ☐ Other/Multiracial

36. Which of the following best describes your gender/sexual orientation?

1 ☐ Heterosexual

2 ☐ Gay/Lesbian

3 ☐ Bi-Sexual

4 ☐ Transgendered

37. What is your current marital status:

1 ☐ Single, never married

2 ☐ Married or living in a "marriage-like" relationship

3 ☐ Divorced

4 ☐ Widowed

38. At any time during your tenure at the largest private law firm with at least 25 attorneys at which you work/worked, what kind of caretaking responsibilities do/did you have for the following people? *(Check one in each row)*

	Primary	Shared	Some, not primary	None
a. Children or Step-Children	1 ☐	2 ☐	3 ☐	4 ☐
b. Someone else's children	1 ☐	2 ☐	3 ☐	4 ☐
c. Elderly parents	1 ☐	2 ☐	3 ☐	4 ☐
d. Other adults	1 ☐	2 ☐	3 ☐	4 ☐

39. **What else would you like to tell us about how your experience in private law firms differed from those of your peers of a different race and/or gender?**

40. **Please identify specific practices that would assist large private law firms to retain women attorneys of color.**

Please look at the last page for more information. ➡

Thank you for completing this survey.
Your responses are valuable.

Please return your questionnaire, including all 8 pages, by:

Mail:
NORC
Project# 6255
1 North State Street, Suite 1600
Chicago, Illinois 60602

or Fax:
(312) 201-4676

E-mail Recruiting Letter Version A

E-Mail Text for survey respondents who expressed an interest in participating in the focus group

Dear [FIRST NAME],

[LAST MONTH], you expressed an interest in participating in a focus group of [WOMEN OF COLOR] attorneys for the ABA Women of Color in the Legal Profession Study. I am writing to provide information about this important research.

NORC, a not-for-profit social science research organization, is conducting a focus group in your area on behalf of the ABA Commission on Women in the Profession. As a follow-up to the survey, we will ask more in-depth questions about your current and past experiences working in a private law firm with 25 or more attorneys. By participating, you will be contributing to research that will help to better understand and address issues facing women attorneys of color like yourself.

During the week of [date], we will be hosting a focus group session in your area from 5:30 PM - 7:30 PM - or at time which meets your availability. Please let us know what days and times are good for you. As a token of our appreciation, participants will be offered $60. Refreshments will be served.

Please be assured that all information you provide will be used for research purposes only, and will be held in the strictest confidence. We will separate all personally identifying information from your responses and report the results from the focus group in summary form only.

We will contact you by telephone in the next few days to answer any question or concerns that you may have. Please feel free to reach us at (312) 759-5095 or ABA-Research@norc.uchicago.edu. You may find additional information about this study and NORC at http://www.norc.uchicago.edu/issues/statmeth7.asp

We look forward to meeting with you!

Sincerely,

M. Mandy Sha
Project Director
NORC, University of Chicago

**E-Mail Text for 1) Survey respondents (who are not aware of the focus groups),
2) Attorneys who are in the frame, but were not sampled for the survey,
3) Referrals who contacted NORC**

Dear Attorney [FIRST NAME] [LAST NAME],

NORC, a not-for-profit social science research organization, is conducting a focus group of [WOMEN OF COLOR] attorneys in your area on behalf of the ABA Commission on Women in the Profession.

As part of the ABA Women of Color in the Legal Profession Study, we will ask more in-depth questions about your current or past experiences working in a private law firm with 25 or more attorneys. By participating, you will be contributing to research that will help to better understand and address issues facing women attorneys of color like yourself.

During the week of [date], we will be hosting a focus group session in your area from 5:30 PM - 7:30 PM - or at time which meets your availability. Please let us know what days and times are good for you. As a token of our appreciation, participants will be offered $60. Refreshments will be served.

Please be assured that all information you provide will be used for research purposes only, and will be held in the strictest confidence. We will separate all personally identifying information from your responses and report the results from the focus group in summary form only.

We will contact you by telephone in the next few days to answer any question or concerns that you may have. Please feel free to reach us at (312) 759-5095 or ABA-Research@norc.uchicago.edu. You may find additional information about this study and NORC at http://www.norc.uchicago.edu/issues/statmeth7.asp

Sincerely,

M. Mandy Sha
Project Director
NORC, University of Chicago

E-Mail Text for Referrals from Attorneys

Dear Attorney [FIRST NAME] [LAST NAME],

[A colleague of yours/ATTORNEY NAME] gave us your contact information so that we may invite you to participate in a research initiative examining the experiences of female attorneys of color.

NORC, a not-for-profit social science research organization, is conducting a focus group of [WOMEN OF COLOR] attorneys in your area on behalf of the ABA Commission on Women in the Profession.

As part of the ABA Women of Color in the Legal Profession Study, we will ask more in-depth questions about your current and past experiences working in a private law firm with 25 or more attorneys. By participating, you will be contributing to research that will help to better understand and address issues facing women attorneys of color like yourself in the legal profession.

During the week of [date], we will be hosting a focus group session in your area from 5:30 PM - 7:30 PM - or at time which meets your availability. Please let us know what days and times are good for you. As a token of our appreciation, participants will be offered $60. Refreshments will be served.

Please be assured that all information you provide will be used for research purposes only, and will be held in the strictest confidence. We will separate all personally identifying information from your responses and report the results from the focus group in summary form only.

We will contact you by telephone in the next few days to answer any question or concerns that you may have. Please feel free to reach us at (312) 759-5095 or ABA-Research@norc.uchicago.edu. You may find additional information about this study and NORC at http://www.norc.uchicago.edu/issues/statmeth7.asp

We look forward to meeting with you!

Sincerely,

M. Mandy Sha
Project Director
NORC, University of Chicago

Informed Consent Payment Forms

Informed Consent Form Version A
For Focus Groups Not Using Web-streaming

Instructions to the Focus Group Participant:

The National Opinion Research Center (NORC) is a non-profit research organization affiliated with the University of Chicago. We are currently conducting a survey on behalf of the American Bar Association Commission on Women in the Profession, to examine issues of interest to Women of Color who have worked at private law firms of at least 25 attorneys during any part of their career in law after graduation.

This focus group is designed to give us the opportunity to get your input and some in-depth discussion of some of the issues examined in that survey. We will be asking you some of the questions in the survey that you may have seen before, as well as a number of follow-up questions that you have not seen. We would like you to discuss them as frankly as possible with the realization that your answers will contribute to our understanding of these issues and will provide the commission with valuable information as they work to improve the work life of Women of Color, and the legal profession in general.

This is not an evaluation of you, or a test of any kind. We will be tape recording this focus group to make sure we have an accurate record of the information you provide and to free the facilitator from constant note-taking. The audio-tapes will be transcribed to facilitate report preparation, but all personal identifiers will be deleted in the transcription. They will be destroyed once the written report (vetted of all identifying information) is completed. Your responses will be confidential and will not be released outside the NORC research team in a form that will allow the identification of individual respondents. No one will know that you participated - including your employer, the ABA, the Commission on Women in the Profession, and/or your former employers.

Please read and sign the following.
This is to verify that I have read the statement above and am willing to participate in the research project described. I also give my permission for my participation in the focus group to be tape recorded for transcription by NORC staff in Chicago. I understand that my recorded and transcribed responses will be kept confidential and that I may withdraw my permission and terminate my participation at any time.

_____
(PLEASE PRINT NAME)

_____
PARTICIPANT SIGNATURE   MONTH DAY YEAR

_____
FACILITATOR SIGNATURE   MONTH DAY YEAR

Instructions to the Focus Group Participant:

The National Opinion Research Center (NORC) is a non-profit research organization affiliated with the University of Chicago. We are currently conducting a survey on behalf of the American Bar Association Commission on Women in the Profession, to examine issues of interest to Women of Color who have worked at private law firms of at least 25 attorneys during any part of their career in law after graduation.

This focus group is designed to give us the opportunity to get your input and some in-depth discussion of some of the issues examined in that survey. We will be asking you some of the questions in the survey that you may have seen before, as well as a number of follow-up questions that you have not seen. We would like you to discuss them as frankly as possible with the realization that your answers will contribute to our understanding of these issues and will provide the commission with valuable information as they work to improve the work life of Women of Color, and the legal profession in general.

This is not an evaluation of you, or a test of any kind. We will be tape recording this focus group to make sure we have an accurate record of the information you provide and to free the facilitator from constant note-taking. We will also be using a web technology called "Active Group" to transmit the sessions via the Internet to authorized NORC staff in Chicago, and stored on a **CD/DVD.** The audio-tapes will be transcribed to facilitate report preparation, but all personal identifiers will be deleted in the transcription. Both the audio-tapes and the **CD/DVD** and will be destroyed once the written report (vetted of all identifying information) is completed. Your responses will be confidential and will not be released outside the NORC research team in a form that will allow the identification of individual respondents. No one will know that you participated -including your employer, the ABA, the Commission on Women in the Profession, and/or your former employers.

Please read and sign the following.
This is to verify that I have read the statement above and am willing to participate in the research project described. I also give my permission for my participation in the focus group to be tape recorded, and videotaped for transmission via the Internet to the NORC staff in Chicago. I understand that my responses will be kept confidential and that I may withdraw my permission and terminate my participation at any time.

_____
(PLEASE PRINT NAME)

_____   └─┴─┘ └─┴─┘ └─┴─┘
PARTICIPANT SIGNATURE   MONTH DAY   YEAR

_____   └─┴─┘ └─┴─┘ └─┴─┘
FACILITATOR SIGNATURE   MONTH DAY   YEAR

Informed Consent Form Version C
for Chicago Focus Group Participants

Instructions to the Focus Group Participant:

The National Opinion Research Center (NORC) is a non-profit research organization affiliated with the University of Chicago. We are currently conducting a survey on behalf of the American Bar Association Commission on Women in the Profession, to examine issues of interest to Women of Color who have worked at private law firms of at least 25 attorneys during any part of their career in law after graduation.

This focus group is designed to give us the opportunity to get your input and some in-depth discussion of some of the issues examined in that survey. We will be asking you some of the questions in the survey that you may have seen before, as well as a number of follow-up questions that you have not seen. We would like you to discuss them as frankly as possible with the realization that your answers will contribute to our understanding of these issues and will provide the commission with valuable information as they work to improve the work life of Women of Color, and the legal profession in general.

This is not an evaluation of you, or a test of any kind. We will be tape recording this focus group to make sure we have an accurate record of the information you provide and to free the facilitator from constant note-taking. The session will be observed by members of the Research Advisory Board from the ABA Commission on Women in the Profession so they can advise NORC about working with the attorney population. Some of them who do not live in Chicago will be using a web technology called "Active Group" to transmit the sessions via the Internet to them. They have signed a Confidentiality and Ethics Agreement that stipulates under no circumstances will they share the information they learned in the focus group session with anyone outside the research team. The session will be stored on a CD/DVD, but they will not receive a copy of the DVD of it. The audio-tapes will be transcribed to facilitate report preparation, but all personal identifiers will be deleted in the transcription. Both the audio-tapes and the CD/DVD will be destroyed once the written report (vetted of all identifying information) is completed. Your responses will be confidential and will not be released outside the NORC research team and the Research Advisory Board in a form that will allow the identification of individual respondents. No one will know that you participated - including your employer, the ABA, and/or your former employers.

Please read and sign the following.
This is to verify that I have read the statement above and am willing to participate in the research project described. I also give my permission for the members of the Research Advisory Board from the ABA Commission on Women in the Profession to observe this session, and for my participation in the focus group to be tape recorded and videotaped for transmission via the Internet to members of the Research Advisory Board that are not in Chicago. I understand that I can request a list of observers if I wish, and my responses will be kept confidential and that I may withdraw my permission and terminate my participation at any time.

_____
(PLEASE PRINT NAME)

_____   └─┴─┘ └─┴─┘ └─┴─┘
PARTICIPANT SIGNATURE   MONTH DAY   YEAR

_____   └─┴─┘ └─┴─┘ └─┴─┘
FACILITATOR SIGNATURE   MONTH DAY   YEAR

LOCATION: _____

I have received $_____ from the NORC Facilitator.

My participation in this study is voluntary. I understand that any information provided by me will be held in strict confidence. My name, address and telephone number will never be associated with any responses provided by me.

_____ |_|_| |_|_| |_|_|
PARTICIPANT INITIALS   MONTH DAY YEAR

_____ |_|_| |_|_| |_|_|
FACILITATOR SIGNATURE   MONTH DAY YEAR

Focus Group Demographics Form

FIRST NAME USED IN FOCUS GROUP _____

The following information will help us understand the make up of our focus groups. This information will be completely confidential and will not be released in individual form. Only totals and averages will be reported and no one outside the research team will have access to the data.

D1: How old were you on your last birthday? |___|___|

D2: Which of the following best describes your race/ethnicity? *(Check One)*

1 ❏ American Indian or Alaska Native
2 ❏ Asian (origins in Far East, South or Southeast Asia)
3 ❏ Black or African-American
4 ❏ Hispanic or Latina
5 ❏ Native Hawaiian or other Pacific Islander
6 ❏ Other/Multiracial → Please specify if you also identify yourself with a racial/ethnic group listed above _____

D3: Do you have a professional or advanced degree other than a J.D.? *(Check One)*

1 ❏ **Yes** → lease specify _____
2 ❏ **No**

D4: Are you currently employed full time? *(Check One)*

1 ❏ **Yes**
2 ❏ **No**

D5: In the largest private law firm in which you ever worked, what was the total number of attorneys firm-wide (*all* offices)?

|___|,|___|___|___|

D6: Which of the following best describes your current employment status? *(Check One)*

1 ❏ an associate or of counsel in a private law firm with at least 25 attorneys
2 ❏ a partner/shareholder in a private law firm with at least 25 attorneys
3 ❏ an associate or of counsel in a private law firm with fewer than 25 attorneys
4 ❏ a partner/shareholder in a private law firm with fewer than 25 attorneys
5 ❏ an in-house attorney in a corporate legal department
6 ❏ an attorney in government, including Department of Justice
7 ❏ an attorney in the nonprofit sector
8 ❏ a judicial clerk
9 ❏ employed but no longer practicing as an attorney
10 ❏ unemployed, retired, or otherwise out of the labor force
11 ❏ not working to stay home to raise my children

Focus Group Protocol

I. Intake and Informed Consent Process

➤ Administer Informed Consent Form (Attachment A)

FACILITATOR: Make sure that focus group subjects read and understand the Informed Consent, and sign and date the form with you. Keep the white copy and give the yellow copy to the subject for her confidential record.

➤ Administer Demographics Information Form (Attachment B)

FACILITATOR: Have focus group subjects fill out the Demographics Information Form in order to gather basic demographic make-up of the group.

➤ Have Participants Create an Alias on Name Tent or Name Tag (If Applicable)

FACILITATOR: Have focus group subjects choose an alias to use throughout the focus group and identity themselves with the alias before speaking. Use a piece of paper to create the name tent.

II. Introduction to the Focus Group

During the last several months, we at NORC conducted a survey for the ABA Commission on Women in the Profession, aimed at examining several issues relevant to the experiences of Women of Color in Law firms. Today, we would like to talk with you further about some of these issues. It is important to know what people in the profession who have worked in law firms think about their experiences in order to form a better understanding of the reactions of attorneys to law firm employment and to help develop a better knowledge of who stays, who leaves, and why.

In today's focus group, we would like to talk with you further about the same issues and ask you to give us your thoughts in a more in-depth fashion to help us better understand your thoughts about your experiences working in a private law firm of at least 25 attorneys.

We understand that you may no longer be working at such a law firm, but for the purposes of this focus group, please think about your experiences during the time when you did work for a law firm of 25 or more attorneys and tell us about those experiences.

III. Icebreaker

Let's get to know each other a little bit before we begin our focus group discussion.

First, please let everyone know the name or alias you will be using tonight. Then, please tell us briefly:

1) the number of years in total you have worked as an attorney in a private law firm with at least 25 attorneys,
2) the size of the law firm or firms (number of attorneys),
3) your position or positions there (e.g. associate, partner, etc.) and practice area, and
4) the diversity of the firm or firms

A) How do you perceive your experiences of being hired, developed and advanced as a women attorney of color in a private law firm? Have they differed from your counterparts that are...

  A- 1. Caucasian female? (And in what ways?)

   [Follow-up if needed]
   (A-1a): Can you give us illustrations from your personal experience?

  A-2. Caucasian men? (And in what ways?)

   [Follow-up if needed]
   (A-2a): Can you give us illustrations from your personal experience?

  A-3. Men of color? (And in what ways?)

   [Follow-up if needed]
   (A-3a): Can you give us illustrations from your personal experience?

B) Next, let's talk about how you perceive your experiences in the workplace in a private law firm.

  Specifically, how did your race/ethnicity and gender affect (either positively or negatively) each of the following aspects of your experience:

   FACILITATOR: This question will "cycle" through the topics about issues in the workplace, and rather than posing them simultaneously.

   During follow-up probes, be sure to:

   1. address these issues for each topic discussed:
      • perceptions of interpersonal relations, issues of harassment, and the general social atmosphere.
      • fairness issues as related to race, gender, or in a sexual context, and how they would have liked to have seen these issues handled.
   2. elicit specific personal examples (not third party observations) on why they feel they were treated differently and what are the root causes of the problems.
   3. ask if they feel this treatment was different in smaller or larger law firms in which they have worked.

  B-1. The hiring process?

  B-2. Career development (i.e. training, mentoring, evaluating)?

  B-3. Advancement?

  B-4. Work allocation and assignments?

  B-5. Evaluations of your performance and pay?

C) What are the top one or two changes that you would like to see implemented in private law firms to address the differences that you experience?

    C-1. What would you like to see that the firm change?

    C-2. Are there things that you could have done differently? Have you observed others who do it well? What can and/or should *individual* attorneys change?

D) With regard to development or training opportunities in your career in a private law firm of at least 25 attorneys, please describe both formal and informal avenues for training and development.

    D-1. Did formal or informal development and training opportunities work best in your experience?

    Were these equally effective? Why or why not?

E) What kinds of support systems outside of private law firms (i.e. professional associations, family, friends, etc.) do you rely upon and use to "survive" and "thrive" in environments where you don't feel supported?

F) Now that you know what the subject of this focus group was, now is the time for you to make any important points that we have failed to bring up for discussion so far.

What have we missed? What key point do you want to make sure we leave with?

V. Wrap-Up

➤ Administer honorarium and Payment Receipt Form (Attachment C).

FACILITATOR: Distribute honorarium. Have recipients initial the payment form with you. Keep the white copy and give the yellow copy to recipient

I. Survey Methodology

Questionnaire Development

The Research Advisory Board drafted a survey questionnaire based on prior studies of gender and race, questions from the ABA membership application, and issues that emerged from ABA conferences. The 40-item questionnaire was developed through a process that involved a one-day meeting, followed by electronic communications and telephone conferences.

The survey included a cover letter from the NORC Project Director explaining the objective of the study and promising participants that their responses would be strictly anonymous. A pre-assigned group identification number indicating whether the attorney was a white man, white woman, woman of color or man of color appeared in the lower left-hand corner of each page of the questionnaire. This was the only identifier that appeared on the document.

Because this was an electronic "paper-and-pencil" survey, special efforts were made to make the questionnaire easy to read and complete. Each question included directions, most questions applied to all respondents and very few offered "Don't know" or "Other—specify" as response options. The survey concluded with two open-ended questions. One question invited participants to describe how their experience in private law firms differed from those of their peers of a different race and/or gender. The other asked respondents to identify specific practices that would help large private law firms retain women attorneys of color.

Sample Design

Attorneys eligible to participate in the survey were identified in two ways. The sample of women attorneys of color was drawn from a list of women attorneys of color who registered their interest and willingness to participate in a survey by going to a Web site hosted by the Commission on Women and providing contact information. The sample of white men, white women, and men of color was randomly drawn from the ABA's Membership Database and restricted to those who had provided an e-mail address on their membership application. Only attorneys who had worked in a private law firm with at least 25 attorneys were eligible to participate in the survey.

Production Training

To prepare for data collection and data processing, NORC developed and conducted three training sessions. The first involved the NORC staff that processed survey questionnaires and e-mail that were returned as undeliverable. They were trained to investigate the reasons why the correspondence could not be delivered (e.g., incorrect address) and to locate respondents. Survey materials were sent to respondents who were successfully located.

The second training was for NORC staff responsible for processing completed questionnaires. Topics included electronically entering the group identification and mode of receipt (mail, fax, etc.) and assigning a receipt identification number. The receipt ID number did not link the completed questionnaire to a specific individual.

In the third training, NORC Computer-Assisted Data Entry (CADE) specialists were trained to enter data from the ABA questionnaire into an electronic database. Quality-assurance procedures were established to ensure the accuracy of data entry.

Survey Data Collection

Prior to data collection, the ABA Commission on Women sent an endorsement letter explaining the importance of the survey to all attorneys in the sample. In October 2004, after the ABA letter was sent, NORC sent attorneys an e-mail with the survey as an attachment. Within a week NORC mailed a business-reply envelope via first-class mail that contained a letter from the NORC project director and a hard copy of the questionnaire. After two weeks, attorneys were sent a reminder e-mail. A month after the first reminder-e-mail, attorneys received a second reminder-e-mail with the survey questionnaire attached. Three weeks after the second reminder-e-mail, respondents received a telephone call and an offer to complete the interview over the telephone. Within a week of the telephone prompting, attorneys were sent a second NORC business-reply envelope with a new letter from the project director, a hard copy of the questionnaire, and a pencil.

Because a group ID was the only identifier affixed to written materials, it was impossible to differentiate between those who had returned a completed questionnaire and those who had not. Therefore, all eligible respondents received all prompts in order to increase the response rate. Respondents who informed NORC that they had completed the survey, those who considered themselves ineligible, and those who refused to participate were excluded from further prompting.

Data Preparation

Quality-control procedures were implemented throughout the data collection and data preparation phases. As NORC received and logged completed questionnaires, the data were recorded in a receipt-control system. Any information that appeared on private mailers was destroyed immediately to protect the respondent's identity. After all questionnaires had been entered into the receipt-control system, data from each questionnaire were entered using the Computer-Assisted Data Entry (CADE) system. Each questionnaire was entered twice, each time by a different data-entry specialist, for 100 percent verification. A supervisor adjudicated differences between the first and second entries by referring to hardcopy questionnaires. Responses to the two open-ended questions at the end of the survey were scanned electronically and delivered to the ABA Commission on Women in password-protected electronic deliveries. The Commission reviewed the pages, had responses typed electronically, and sent the typed entries back to NORC without any individual identifiers.

Cleaning the data involved reviewing frequencies and checking for inconsistencies in the data. NORC could not retrieve data for missing or incomplete values because questionnaires could not be traced back to individual respondents. Out-of-scope cases were identified during the data-cleaning process; 72 questionnaires were completed and returned by attorneys who turned out to be ineligible or out of scope (for

example, attorneys who never worked in law firms with at least 25 attorneys). Verbatim responses from the open-ended survey questions were presented in summary form by question and sample type (i.e., women of color, men of color, white women and white men) and delivered to NORC for initial analysis.

II. Focus Group Methodology

The focus groups in this study were conducted after the survey was complete and were intended to be used as a qualitative tool for gathering in-depth information about the career experiences and trajectories covered in the survey, from the perspective of women of color. Focus groups were restricted to women of color.

Protocol Development

Focus group participants were asked first to describe their experiences in hiring, development and advancement, and to compare their experiences with those of their counterparts. Topics included training, work allocation and assignments, salary, mentoring and evaluations of performance. They were asked next to describe the positive and negative effects of gender and their specific race on their experiences in law firms and to compare their experiences with those of white men, white women and men of color. They were then asked about training and development opportunities in law firms and changes that private law firms could make that would enhance the career success of women of color in law firms as well as support they received from family, friends, and professional associations. (The focus group protocol can be found in Appendix A.)

Facilitator Qualifications and Training

NORC used experienced focus group facilitators with strong backgrounds in the social sciences and proficiencies in issues of race and gender based on academic training and/or personal experience. Facilitators attended an in-person training on the protocol used in the study, which was also attended by NORC research staff, members of the Research Advisory Board, and representatives from the ABA Commission on Women. Facilitators did not have a legal background, so their training included legal definitions, common career paths for attorneys, and characteristics of private law firms. They were also briefed on the principles and efficacy of focus groups as an exploratory tool. Facilitators had opportunities to practice administering the focus group protocol during the group training and during individual sessions with NORC professional staff and/or members of the Research Advisory Board.

Recruitment of Focus Group Participants

NORC recruited for the focus groups African-American, Hispanic/Latina, Asian-American, Native American, and biracial/multiracial women attorneys who had worked in private law firms with 25 attorneys or more at some point in their career after graduating from law school. Eight to 10 women were recruited for each focus group, and no more than one respondent from a firm was invited to attend. Attorneys were recruited from three sources: the sample of survey respondents, attorneys who did not participate in the survey but indicated their interest in the study through a Web site sponsored by the ABA Commission on Women, and referrals from sampled respondents and other legal networks, such as national and local minority legal associations. NORC sent potential focus group participants an e-mail letter tailored to each recruitment source. Attorneys were then contacted by telephone to conduct an eligibility screening interview.

Conducting the Focus Groups

Each focus group was held on a weekday evening for two hours during March and the first week of April 2005. All groups convened at professional focus group research facilities. During the first half hour, participants were offered refreshments and asked to sign a document giving informed consent for their participation. The facilitators then guided participants through the focus group protocol. When the session ended, participants were offered a $60 honorarium and asked to sign a payment receipt form.

The first focus group was conducted in Chicago. It served as a pilot group and was used to refine and improve the administration of the protocol. The research staff at NORC observed all focus groups from behind a two-way mirror or via Web-streaming technology that transmitted the session over the Internet.

Debriefing the Facilitators

Focus group facilitators were debriefed after all focus groups were completed. They were asked to provide information that could help in the interpretation of focus group data and to compare and contrast each focus group. The debriefing covered group dynamics and interactions among focus group participants, the accuracy of transcripts, the effectiveness of the protocol (in terms of length, complexity, and flow), strengths and weaknesses in the discussion, and participants' reactions to questions about the combined impact of race and gender on career dynamics.

III. Protection of Human Subjects

Because there are so few women attorneys of color in medium-sized and large private firms, detailed procedures to protect participants from being identified and descriptions of the survey and focus group protocols were submitted to NORC's Institutional Review Board (IRB) and were approved. NORC staff signed statements confirming that they understood NORC's confidentiality and professional ethics, and pledged to uphold those standards.

The data delivered to the ABA Commission on Women identified respondents with a group ID only (one for each race/gender group). A unique case identifier was assigned to completed questionnaires for the exclusive purpose of receipt control. This identifier could not be traced back to a respondent's name or other personal information. The ABA Commission on Women did not receive hardcopy questionnaires except for a page of verbatim responses stripped of any identifying information.

No one participated in the focus groups without having first read, understood, and signed an Informed Consent Form. When Web-streaming technology was used to enable NORC researchers in Chicago to observe the focus group, participating attorneys were briefed on its use and asked for their consent. All observers signed a non-disclosure agreement with NORC prior to observing the group.

In conformance with standard practice, all hardcopy data, including worksheets, CDs and audiotapes, were stored in locked file cabinets at NORC under the direct supervision of the project staff. Access to data with identifiers was strictly limited to project personnel and stored on secure password-protected computers in locked offices.

Employment Status

The current employment status of attorneys who responded to the survey is shown in Table A. Most attorneys, regardless of race/ethnicity or gender, were employed in private law firms of at least 25 attorneys.

Table A: Employment Status of Survey Respondents

Current Employment Status	Women of color	Men of color	White Women	White men
	(N=437)	(N=132)	(N=194)	(N=157)
Associate/of counsel, law firm with 25 attorneys or more	41%	23%	19%	20%
Partner/shareholder, law firm with 25 attorneys or more	12%	28%	46%	52%
Associate/of counsel, law firm with fewer than 25 attorneys	4%	7%	3%	3%
Partner/shareholder, law firm with fewer than 25 attorneys	4%	13%	9%	13%
In-house (Corporation)	14%	16%	11%	5%
Government (including DOJ or judicial clerk)	11%	5%	2%	3%
Nonprofit	4%	2%	1%	1%
Employed, no longer practicing law	7%	5%	5%	3%
Unemployed or retired	1%	0%	1%	0%
Not working, raising children	1%	0%	1%	0%
Did not answer	1%	1%	3%	1%

Forty-one percent of women of color in the survey were associates or attorneys of counsel compared to 23% of men of color, 19% of white women and 20% of white men. Only 12% of women of color were partners or shareholders compared to 28% of men of color, 46% of white women and 52% of white men.

Twenty-nine percent of women attorneys of color were employed by the government, nonprofit organizations or were in-house counsel in corporations compared to 23% of men of color, 14% of white women, and 9% of white men. Less than 1% of attorneys in the survey were home full-time rearing their children; these attorneys were women.

Education

Most respondents in the survey went to first- or second-tier law schools. As shown in Table B, 57% of women attorneys of color graduated from a first-tier law school compared to 46% of men of color, 40% of white women, and 52% of white men. However, in terms of class rank, white women and white men were nearly twice as likely to have been in Law Review or the Order of the Coif as women or men attorneys of color. Twenty-five percent of men attorneys of color were below the 50th percentile in law school compared to 15% of women of color, 6% of white women and 5% of white men. Few attorneys in the survey worked as a judicial clerk after graduating from law school, but 23% of women of color, 21% of men of color, 17% of white women and 18% of white men did so.

Table B: Educational Background and Clerkship Experience

	Women of color	Men of color	White women	White men
School Rank	(N=437)	(N=132)	(N=194)	(N=157)
Tier 1 (top 20)	57%	46%	40%	52%
Tier 2 (21-40)	19%	24%	23%	17%
Tier 3 (41 and below)	11%	10%	9%	13%
Did not answer	13%	20%	28%	18%
Class Rank	(N=437)	(N=132)	(N=194)	(N=157)
Law Review/Honors, Order of the Coif	22%	24%	42%	43%
1st quartile (not Law Review/Honors)	16%	16%	26%	28%
2nd quartile (26th-50th percentile)	39%	32%	23%	21%
3rd quartile (51st-75th percentile)	12%	21%	5%	4%
4th quartile (76th-100th percentile)	3%	4%	1%	1%
Did not answer	8%	4%	2%	3%
Worked as Judicial Clerk	(N=437)	(N=132)	(N=194)	(N=157)
Yes	23%	21%	17%	18%
No	77%	79%	83%	82%

Age and Years of Practice

Overall, the women attorneys of color in the survey were younger than their counterparts and had spent fewer years practicing law. As shown in Table C, 50% of the women of color in the survey were 35 years of age or younger, as were only 11% of white women and 8% of white men. Half of the white women and white men in the survey were between 46 and 60 years of age, as were only 11% of women of color.

Table C: Age, Years Since Law School Graduation, and Years of Legal Practice

	Women of color	Men of color	White Women	White men
Age	(N=437)	(N=132)	(N=194)	(N=157)
35 years or less	50%	21%	11%	8%
36 to 45 years	38%	29%	34%	17%
46 to 60 years	11%	38%	52%	52%
Older than 60	1%	12%	4%	24%
Years Since Law School Graduation	(N=437)	(N=132)	(N=194)	(N=157)
10 years or less	63%	33%	23%	15%
11 to 25 years	33%	46%	54%	34%
26 to 45 years	4%	18%	22%	40%
More than 45 years ago	<1%	3%	<1%	10%
Years Spent Practicing Law	(N=437)	(N=132)	(N=194)	(N=157)
10 years or less	71%	40%	28%	18%
11 to 25 years	26%	45%	54%	39%
26 to 45 years	3%	12%	18%	34%
More than 45 years	0%	3%	0%	8%

These age differences are consistent with differences among attorneys in the number of years since law school graduation and the number of years spent practicing law. Nearly two-thirds of women of color graduated within the past 10 years, as did only 15% of white men. Half of the white men in the survey graduated from law school more than 25 years ago, as did only 4% of women of color. White women and men of color had more similar profiles in terms of years since graduation from law school.

Seventy-one percent of women of color had practiced law for 10 years or less, compared to 40% of men of color, 28% of white women, and 18% of white men. Just over one-third of white men had practiced law for 26 to 45 years; they were presumably at the peak or end of their careers in law. Only 3% of women attorneys of color in the survey were at a similar stage in their careers.

Law Firm Experience and Number of Employers

As shown in Table D, a larger percentage of women of color worked in firms with more than 450 lawyers and in firms that employed 800 or more attorneys than did their counterparts. Eighty percent of the women attorneys of color were associates, as were 51% of men of color, 43% of white women, and 27% of white men. Only 10% of women of color were equity or capital partners or held a leadership position within the firm compared to 62% of white men, 40% of white women and 38% of men of color.

Table D: Law Firm Experience and Number of Employers

	Women of color	Men of color	White women	White men
No. Attorneys Firmwide at Largest Firm	(N=437)	(N=132)	(N=194)	(N=157)
25 to 100	19%	33%	21%	28%
101 to 250	17%	22%	26%	26%
251 to 450	18%	21%	24%	17%
451 to 800	22%	12%	15%	16%
More than 800	24%	12%	14%	14%
Highest Rank at Largest Firm	(N=437)	(N=132)	(N=194)	(N=157)
Firm or dept. leadership	4%	17%	20%	43%
Equity/capital partner	6%	21%	20%	19%
Associate	81%	51%	43%	27%
All other ranks	5%	10%	16%	11%
Did not answer	<1%	2%	<1%	0%
Years at Firm, > 25 Attorneys	(N=437)	(N=132)	(N=194)	(N=157)
10 years or less	90%	67%	52%	42%
11 to 25 years	9%	26%	41%	39%
26 to 40 years	<1%	6%	7%	17%
> 40 years	0%	1%	0%	3%
No. Employers	(N=437)	(N=132)	(N=194)	(N=157)
1 to 2	53%	38%	47%	44%
3 to 5	40%	49%	41%	46%
6 or more	7%	14%	11%	10%

Ninety percent of women attorneys of color had spent 10 years or less at a firm of 25 attorneys or more. Sixty-seven percent of men of color, 52% of white women, and 42% of white men had similarly short tenures. Just over half of the women attorneys of color had one or two employers. Only 7% of women attorneys of color had six or more employers, compared to 10% to 14% of the other groups.

Marital Status and Sexual Orientation

As shown in Table E, most respondents were married or living with a partner, but fewer women of color were married compared to the other groups. More than one-third of the women attorneys of color had never married compared to 14% of men attorneys of color, 8% of white women, and 6% of white men. Divorce rates were also higher among women (8% of women of color and 10% of white women) compared to the men in the sample (5% of men of color and white men). The majority of all groups in the sample described themselves as heterosexual.

Table E: Marital Status and Sexual Orientation

	Women of color	Men of color	White women	White men
Marital Status	(N=437)	(N=132)	(N=194)	(N=157)
Single, never married	35%	14%	8%	6%
Married or living with partner	56%	80%	81%	89%
Divorced or widowed	8%	5%	10%	5%
Did not answer	1%	1%	<1%	<1%
Sexual Orientation	(N=437)	(N=132)	(N=194)	(N=157)
Heterosexual	96%	93%	97%	97%
Gay/lesbian/bi-sexual	3%	4%	2%	3%
Did not answer	1%	3%	1%	0%

Caveats in Interpreting the Data

Two considerations should be taken into account when interpreting the findings in this study. The first pertains to the sampling strategy used and the other pertains to the demographic profile of survey respondents.

Two different sampling strategies were used in the survey. The sample of men attorneys of color and white men and women attorneys was a probability sample. The sample of women of color was a non-probability sample. In a probability sample, every person who could potentially be included in the sample has a known non-zero probability of inclusion. Sampling error, the degree to which a sample (of lawyers) may differ from the population (of lawyers), can be computed from a probability sample. Sampling error is usually described by the phrase "plus or minus." In non-probability samples, the degree to which the sample differs from the population remains unknown. Because the sample of women of color was created through a process of self-selection, the degree to which these survey respondents reflect the characteristics, attitudes, and experiences of the overall population of women attorneys of color is unknown. If there is a bias in the sample, we would expect that the women of color who volunteered to participate might have stronger feelings, a greater consciousness of race and/or gender, or, perhaps, more negative experiences than women attorneys of color who chose not to enroll in the survey. Despite these caveats, this study represents the first attempt to systematically sample women attorneys of color and to compare their experiences with those of men attorneys of color and white men and women attorneys.

It is also important to note that the women attorneys of color who participated in the survey were younger than their white counterparts and had spent fewer years practicing law. This may explain in part why a higher percentage of women of color in the survey were associates compared to white women and men. It also suggests that there may be "generational" differences in the career experiences of women of color and those of their white counterparts. The women of color in the survey, for the most part, are in the ascendancy of their careers and are of childbearing age, in sharp contrast to the majority of white men in the sample, who are at the peak of their careers or nearing the age of retirement.